Rethinking Religion

Finding a Place for Religion in a Modern, Tolerant, Progressive, Peaceful and Science-affirming World

Barbara O'Brien

D1398144

Published by Ten Directions

ISBN/EAN13: 0692224505 / 9780692224502

The paperback edition is available as an Amazon Kindle edition:

Kindle Edition ISBN: 9780692219461

You may contact the author by email at **mahabarbara@gmail.com**.

Printed by CreateSpace, Charleston SC, USA

To my teacher, Tokudo Ji-on Susan Postal

1940-2014

who encouraged me to be a dragon.

Table of Contents

Preface, 1

Chapter 1: The Religion Problem, 2

Chapter 2: Defining Religion, 9

Chapter 3: Spiritual Is Religious, 19

Chapter 4: God and Existence, 38

Chapter 5: Iron Age Morality in a Postmodern World, 52

Chapter 6: The Crazy Scripture in the Attic, 78

Chapter 7: True Believers and Mass Movements, 102

Chapter 8: Religion and Violence, 121

Chapter 9: The Wisdom of Doubt, 153

Endnotes, 174

Preface

This book is about religion. But I promise I will not argue that everyone should be religious (or not), nor will I attempt to change your personal religious orientation, whatever that is.

However, I do intend to challenge your ideas about religion, whatever they are.

This book is a proposal to rethink religion so that our definitions are both more accurate and more inclusive of the variety of religious experience around the world. It also is an argument that there is a way to be religious *and* modern, open minded, progressive, appreciative of science, tolerant, and a peaceful global citizen of the 21st century. And it's also an argument that there's a lot about religion that is hurting humanity more than helping, and religious people especially must address this.

This book is written from a progressive perspective. I very much hope religious conservatives will read it, too, and not dismiss it out of hand. However, I am speaking primarily to other progressives — atheists, agnostics, religious and "spiritual but not religious" — because I think we have common cause if not common understanding.

Although I draw considerably on personal experience, this is not a book *about* my personal experience. I am not ready to write *that* book yet.

If you enjoy *this* book and think it has some value, please tell your friends about it. I am not a person of means, by any stretch, and I have no publicity or promotion budget.

I can be emailed at mahabarbara@gmail.com. I'm not good at responding to emails, though. If email doesn't work, you can leave a comment on my personal blog, The Mahablog, at http://www.mahablog.com. I also write the Buddhism section at About.com.

This book is dedicated to my Zen teacher, Ji-on Susan Postal, who died of cancer while I was writing it. But I also want to say thank you to Mahablog readers and also to my brother and sister zennies of Empty Hand Zen Center, for their encouragement.

Barbara Hoetsu O'Brien
May 2014

I

I The Religion Problem

The whole thing is so patently infantile, so foreign to reality, that to anyone with a friendly attitude to humanity it is painful to think that the great majority of mortals will never be able to rise above this view of life. It is still more humiliating to discover how a large number of people living today, who cannot but see that this religion is not tenable, nevertheless try to defend it piece by piece in a series of pitiful rearguard actions. — Sigmund Freud, *Civilization and Its Discontents* (1930)

In recent decades the "pitiful rearguard actions" have turned violent. Much, if not most, of the ongoing mass bloodshed in the world today has a connection to religion, in one way or another, and followers of most of the world's major religions are represented as both victims and perpetrators.

In January 2014 the Pew Research Religion and Public Life Project released a report saying that religious violence around the globe had reached a six-year high. [i] Yet a number of historians, sociologists and other smart people have declared that we're living in the most peaceful time in human history, overall. Given the persistence of religion-related violence, it's hard to escape the conclusion that there's something about religion that is stoking the hate flames, somehow.

I'm religious myself, and I have no intention of launching into an anti-religion screed. But neither do I intend to write pro-religion apologia. It's time for the religious to look at religion more critically and admit to what's gone wrong with it.

Later in this book I'm going to look at religious violence and the factors that continue to churn tribal animosities that explode into warfare. Eliminating religion isn't necessarily going to lead to world peace, although it might help. But violence isn't the only way in which religion is trying to drag civilization back to more barbaric times.

In the latter part of the 20th century, religious and political conservatives joined forces in the United States and, drunk with self-righteousness and certitude, launched a campaign of take-no-prisoners partisan politics that has brought the nation to the brink of utter dysfunction. Today we are saddled with a powerful faction of fanatics who "believe in" their backward political ideology in the same way they "believe in" religious dogma. Compromise, necessary to a functioning representative government, is apostasy; they see their political opponents as agents of dark and unholy forces who must be crushed by any means.

More than 150 years after the publication of Darwin's *Origin of Species*, science teachers are still fighting to teach evolution properly in public schools. Religion sometimes is used to prop up climate change denialism, which has hamstrung our ability to address a real threat to our planet. Nearly 50 years after *Griswold v. Connecticut* and more than 40 years after *Roe v. Wade* the political-religious Right has succeeded in restricting access to birth control as well as abortion for vulnerable low-income women in conservative states.

Considering all this, it's tempting to think that the world would be a better place without religion. And maybe it would. Or maybe all the tribalism, bigotry, and fear would just find another container.

The question is, does religion have anything positive to offer the 21st century (and beyond)? Or is it a vestige of the Iron Age that ought to be contained in museums?

More critically, is it even possible to be religious and also be a rational and entirely modern participant in 21st-century civilization? Is it possible to live a devotional, religious life today without denying science or otherwise being assimilated by some religious-authoritarian Borg?

I say the answer to this question depends on how you conceptualize and define religion.

* * *

My proposal to rethink religion is not to water it down or re-tool it into something more like philosophy. Rather, I propose we dig deeply into its roots to rediscover what religion *is*. I say "rediscover" because I honestly think we've forgotten. Much of today's popular religiosity is an infantile caricature of religion that many theologians and clergy of the past wouldn't recognize as religion at all.

We can't simply restore the "old time religion," however, because what "worked" for our ancestors, especially those who lived before the age of scientific reason, simply won't work for us. We understand ourselves and everything else in an entirely different way, and there's no going back.

The ascension of science not only changed what we know to be true, but how we understand truth itself. Before the age of scientific reason, *truth* was about meaning, not facts. For example, written accounts of real events often were embellished with fantastical details that couldn't possibly have happened, but which symbolically expressed what the event meant to the writer and his contemporaries. And to people who lived a thousand years ago, those fantastical embellishments were *truth*.

The English word *truth* comes from the Old English *triew,* which meant something like "faithful." The word didn't mean "factual" or "accurate," as in the opposite of "lie," until the 16th century or so. Before that, supernatural story embellishments, or fantastical accounts of an actual event, were accepted as truth if the stories expressed what people felt about the event or how they understood its significance.

And if you vouched for your friend's truth, you were saying he was a stand-up guy who would come through for you when you need him. Whether he really truly caught a 50-pound trout with a piece of string and a paper clip, as he claimed, was beside the point.

The conflation of truth with factuality, or with phenomena that can be objectively verified and empirically tested, was a process that began in western civilization in the 15th century or so. And in a few more centuries it came to pass that people no longer looked to myths and metaphors for meaning, and anything that wasn't factual was considered untrue. This posed a great challenge to religion, with its pre-scientific age scriptures written in the language of myth.

And this is a challenge that much of religion has failed.

This failure is not limited to Christianity, but the damage is more apparent in Christianity than in some other traditions. Very simply, many people *wanted* to believe in God and other doctrines as "truth," but they had lost the ability to appreciate the intuitive truth and meaning of allegory and myth. The result is scriptural literalism, or the insistence that scriptures and doctrines must be literally and factually true, not metaphorical, allegorical, or mythical.

Not all religious sects have embraced literalism, but even the non-literal often struggle to express their ancient truths in ways that are meaningful to modern thinkers.

Literalism is a relatively new way to understand religion, and the result of literalism is that religion is rendered into nothing but a superstitious belief system. And today a great many people are absolutely certain that's all religion is.

I argue that religion was, is, and can be something else entirely, a "something else" that might offer much to us today if we could re-learn how to understand it and express it.

* * *

Modernity teaches us that reason alone is the key to knowledge and wisdom, and all other modes of understanding are "magical thinking" or "superstition." But the truth is that none of us are as rational as we think we are. Even the brightest among us are being jerked around by our subconscious minds more than we realize; even the most rational and educated are navigating the world in a fog of projection and cognitive bias.

How do we know this? Science is telling us this, for one thing. For example, there is a growing body of evidence that most of our decisions, opinions and moral judgments are really being made by our emotions or intuition, and we use reason largely to explain to ourselves how we reached our decision or formed our opinion.

Entre nous — Yes, I'm sure that doesn't apply to *you*, but it certainly does apply to everyone *else*, doesn't it?

For a more thorough explanation, see *The Righteous Mind: Why Good People Are Divided by Politics and Religion* by social psychologist Jonathan Haidt (Pantheon Books, 2012). Haidt explains in detail the many ways people have been tested to reveal that reason plays only a supporting role in why we actually think as we do. Most of our decision- and opinion-making processes are taking place on subconscious levels.

I say reason is grand, and the world could do with more critical thinking, not less. But the reach of reason is far more limited than we might assume. Further, in embracing reason over all, humankind appears to have lost touch with other ways of perceiving, understanding, and experiencing that are just as "real," and just as natural and valid, but which can't always be explained with words or subjected to empirical testing.

In short, most of us are just as blinkered and oblivious to reality as our superstitious ancestors; it's just that we're blinkered and oblivious in new and modern ways.

Where does religion come into this? I propose that religion really does have a role to play in modern life if we can pry it away from literalism. Religion *can* be a means to extend the reach of insight and expand awareness beyond the boundaries of the limited self. And it can still do what it has always done, in myriad ways — guide us in our experience of living and dying.

I sincerely believe it's possible for the not-literalist religious to reclaim the *truth* of religion and make religion meaningful and relevant to 21st century life. And it can do this without denying science or truncating critical thinking skills. To this end, I propose a re-thinking that is both old and new. What is old are core traditions of practice and insight, elements of which stretch back into prehistory. What is new will be how we creatures of modernity might perceive, experience and manifest this insight.

And to understand what I'm saying it may be necessary to completely jettison everything you think you know about religion, whether you are for it or against it.

* * *

Lots of people today genuinely hate religion, and I can't say I blame them. Most of religion represented in popular culture and in news media is backward and stupid. That's because a lot of modern religion *is* backward and stupid. And there's nothing more annoying than backward, stupid people who insist everyone else should believe as they do.

And let me be clear that I don't think everyone *has* to be religious. Some of us are drawn to some sort of religion or spiritual practice. Some of us aren't. It's an individual thing. In my perfect imaginary world, all forms of proselytizing would end, and all forms of religion would be a personal commitment, freely chosen or rejected, that is no one else's damn business. I concede mine is a minority view, though.

People are drawn to religion for many reasons. Some of those reasons are psychologically healthy, and some aren't. By the same token, some religious paths can help one find peace and sanity, while others are likely to make you buggier than you were when you started. And sometimes it's not the religion itself, but how one relates to it, that makes the difference between the saintly and the assimilated.

Throughout human history religion has served as the glue holding communities and societies together, and it also has given authority to tyrants and moral cover for atrocities. It has comforted and terrified; it has inspired and corrupted. In short, it is an expression of the best and worst of humanity.

I believe it's possible to preserve and enhance the "best" while scaling back the "worst." And if we do that, perhaps religion might finally get to work on its promise of peace on earth.

Doing that will require — surprise! — applying at least some reason and critical thinking skills to religion and the behaviors it inspires. By examining religion in a more dispassionate and disinterested light perhaps we can better understand how and why religions become destructive, and make adjustments.

This book amounts to a proposal for how we may proceed.

* * *

General notes on the chapters ahead: Part of the purpose of this book is to explore the possibilities of being religious (*and* spiritual!) as a modern, tolerant, progressive, peaceful and science-friendly citizen of the world. It isn't that hard, you know. Lots of people of many religious traditions are doing it already. And this can be done without cherry-picking doctrine or re-writing scripture, although it does require *relating* to doctrine and scripture in a way foreign to fundamentalism.

Unfortunately, such people are rarely the ones who get interviewed on the TeeVee.

I'm also going to argue that much of religion as it currently exists is hurting humanity more than helping, and it ought to be retired. Speaking as a religious person myself, I think religion is worth salvaging, but only if we can come to terms with why it so easily becomes a tool for regression, repression and oppression.

What *is* the connection between religion and violence? This must be understood clearly. Glib answers and knee-jerk assumptions won't get us anywhere.

And finally, I will urge that we stop thinking of religion as something entire societies and nations must be indoctrinated or coerced into following.

However, I'm *not* going to argue for scuttling the established religious traditions so that "religion" becomes a buffet of beliefs and practices one may choose from to suit one's fancy. Each of the world's great religions has something unique and precious to offer, and I'd vote to keep their integrity preserved.

I'm not writing for academics or theologians, but for intelligent and thoughtful people who don't have a graduate degree in religious studies (neither do I). I assure you, I have no interest in converting anyone to my particular religious perspective. For the record, I was raised Christian but now practice Soto Zen Buddhism, a tradition that discourages proselytizing. I will refer to Buddhism frequently, but I'm not trying to sell it.

As I've been working on this book I realized that I refer to Christianity a lot. I hope I don't come across as picking on Christians in particular. It's just that I know Christianity well enough that I feel comfortable offering opinions about it. If it frustrates you that I don't criticize Islam or Judaism as much, it's partly because I don't know those traditions as well. But let's face it — Christianity is the 800-pound gorilla of western religion, so to speak. And you may notice I'm not always sparing of Buddhism.

Regarding my use of the word *fundamentalism* — I understand that Christian fundamentalism originally was a movement in American Christianity that proposed a particular set of doctrines. Sometimes I use the word in that sense. But sometimes I also use it in a broader sense, as explained by religion scholar Karen Armstrong in her book *The Battle for God: Fundamentalism in Judaism, Christianity and Islam* (Knopf/HarperCollins, 2000). She defined fundamentalism as a "militant religiosity" that is a "reaction against and a rejection of modern Western society." Fundamentalism in this sense has infected religious traditions around the globe, not just Christianity.

In its most extreme forms, I say fundamentalism isn't even religion. It's more of a social pathology that expresses itself as religion. However, the scriptural literalism that is the trademark of fundamentalism can be found in a broad spectrum of religion today, and it's a serious problem.

Another word I use sometimes is *metaphysics*, which I define in the broadest sense, as *any* exploration of or inquiry into the fundamental nature of existence. I keep bumping into writers who seem to think metaphysics deals with the supernatural, and use the word in that sense, and that ain't necessarily so.

Note that some of the views expressed herein are not necessarily mine. For example, I will sometimes speak of God as if I believe that God exists. I don't, at least by any common definition of "believe." Or "God." Or "exist."

Make of that what you will

2   Defining Religion

> There is hardly a word in the religious language, both theological and popular, which is subject to more misunderstandings, distortions and questionable definitions than the word "faith." — Paul Tillich, *Dynamics of Faith* (1957)

Late in 2003 the Pew Research Center for the People and the Press reported that "religious" people tend to vote Republican and "non-religious" people tend to vote Democratic. But how does one measure "religious"?

According to survey data, Pew's criteria were (1) belief in the power of prayer, (2) belief in a final Day of Judgment, and (3) belief beyond doubt in the existence of God.

Now, consider that His Holiness the 14th Dalai Lama would fail this test. Buddhist doctrines do not include the God of monotheism or a Day of Judgment, and His Holiness wrote not long ago that "prayer cannot match the achievements of, for instance, modern science."[ii]

We're talking about a guy in his 70s who has not only been a celibate, ordained monk almost from infancy, but I understand he gets up at 3:30 every morning so he can put in a few hours of meditation and ritual before breakfast. If that's not religious, what is?

This exemplifies the degree to which our definition of "religion" in the early 21st century West has been degraded into nothing more than a kind of supernatural ideology mostly based on the most conservative and dogmatic parts of Christianity. Meanwhile, activist atheists love to knock religious faith by quoting Ambrose Bierce — faith is "belief without evidence" — overlooking the facts that Bierce was writing satire, that *faith* as religious people use the word is not always a synonym for *belief*, and that not all religions are primarily about believing things.

But it's hard to blame them, because contemporary Christianity especially appears to have signed on to the notion that "religion" equals "faith" and "faith" equals "belief." But that is not true of most of the world's religions, and indeed, it didn't use to be true of Christianity.

This is not to say that belief has no place in religion. I acknowledge that religious traditions function within a kind of conceptual or doctrinal framework that proposes or accepts God, or Brahman, or immortal souls, or samsara. However, in many traditions merely believing that these things are factually "real" is pointless. The concepts that make up the box are understood in many ways beside *literal*.

The view among many religious people in the West, that everything that one reads in scriptures must be accepted as literal fact, actually is relatively new. Within many Asian religions the idea that scriptures must only be *literal* truth would be considered weird, even ignorant.

Some religions *are* mostly supernatural belief systems, but in others belief plays only a supporting or provisional role. In many schools of Buddhism, for example, doctrines are regarded as something like hypotheses to be tested, not as "facts" that must be believed in because somebody says so.[iii]

Many religious people, East and West, see doctrines as provisional teachings that fall short of an ineffable absolute, whatever that is. I tend to see the doctrines of most religions, including mine, as what Buddhists call *upaya* — expedient means — or something like learning aids that point to truths beyond the reach of conceptualization. For this reason other people's religious beliefs don't bother me as long as the beliefs aren't causing them to do harm. It's all upaya.

In many Asian traditions it is accepted that understanding of doctrine will — and, in fact, should — change over time, because the *practice* of that tradition will enlarge one's capacity to understand it. A beginner's understanding of Brahma or Buddha *will* be considerably different from a master's, and everybody's okay with that.

Indeed it's often the case that doctrines mostly function as markers on whatever spiritual path that tradition has laid out. They are guides to the truth, not the truth in itself. In those traditions, simply accepting some prefabricated package of beliefs as "true" is hardly religion at all.

There are arguments for some kind of practice leading to greater understanding in western theology as well. Saint Anshelm's *fides quaerens intellectum* — faith seeking understanding — is one example, I'd say, but there are others.

I'm speaking in generalities here, and there are many exceptions to what I'm saying. But my point is that in the West our contemporary ideas about religion have become rigid and narrow, and much that used to be accepted as "religion" is left out. We have stuffed religion into a very tiny conceptual box.

* * *

What then is religion? In the West, most people appear to base the definition of religion on Christianity. This is understandable; Christianity is so pervasive in the West no westerner can avoid being exposed to it, including those who would prefer it left them alone. For many westerners it's the only religion they know anything about.

Christianity shares historical roots with Judaism and Islam, and these three traditions are sometimes called the "Abrahamic" religions, because they all claim the Prophet Abraham as a patriarch. Because these three traditions share historical, cultural and doctrinal roots, their conceptual frameworks share some similarities. For example, they are all monotheistic. They all have written scriptures thought to be the Word of God and invested with great authority. Their main concern, in one way or another, is the relationship between man and God.

Westerners often assume that all "religions" share all three of those traits. In fact, outside of Abrahamism, most *don't*. Some religious traditions don't share *any* of them.

The Abrahamic model gives us most of our dictionary definitions of religion, such as "the belief in and worship of a superhuman controlling power, especially a personal God or gods." Or, "the belief in a god or in a group of gods; an organized system of beliefs, ceremonies, and rules used to worship a god or a group of gods."

However, this Abrahamic conceptual framework leaves out pretty much everything else in the world that usually is referred to as "religion," to one degree or another. Sikhism is monotheistic and has some general commonalities with the Abrahamic model, I think. But most of the other religions of Asia have entirely different conceptual frameworks to which the English language dictionary definitions do not apply.

* * *

You might remember that back in 2010 it was learned that golfer Tiger Woods was frequently unfaithful to his wife. This caused Fox News personality Britt Hume to opine —

> The extent to which he can recover seems to me depends on his faith. . . . He is said to be a Buddhist. I don't think that faith offers the kind of redemption and forgiveness offered by the Christian faith. My message to Tiger is, "Tiger turn to the Christian faith and you can make a total recovery and be a great example to the world."

With considerable self-discipline I refrained from calling Mr. Hume an ignorant sot, and instead wrote (among other things),

> Mr. Hume is right, in a sense, that Buddhism doesn't offer re-
> demption and forgiveness in the same way Christianity does.
> Buddhism has no concept of sin; therefore, redemption and
> forgiveness in the Christian sense are meaningless in Bud-
> dhism. Forgiveness is important, but it is approached differ-
> ently in Buddhism, and I'll get to that in a bit.[iv]

Naturally, Fox News's Bill O'Reilly and some guy named Peter Sprigg from the conservative Family Research Council pulled my words out of context and claimed *I had agreed with Britt Hume*, and declared that even a Buddhist admits that Buddhism falls short in the redemption of sins department. But to me, this is a meaningless technicality. Within the Buddhist conceptual framework, the phrase "redemption of sins" is nonsensical. What O'Reilly and Sprigg said is a bit like claiming aspirin is superior to algebra because aspirin will relieve your headache, and algebra won't.

Let me add that I also got slammed by some other Buddhists for saying Buddhism has no concept of sin. The word "sin" does crop up in Buddhist commentaries written in English, although I'm not sure it has many Asian language equivalents, and its use generally is discouraged in western Zen. I argue that what Buddhists mean by "sin" is different from how the word is understood in Abrahamism, but I may be speaking more for Zen than for other schools of Buddhism in this matter. Still, in Buddhism, nobody needs to be "redeemed."

Sometimes when westerners do see that the Abrahamic framework doesn't apply to an Asian religion, they conclude the Asian religion isn't a religion at all, which happens a lot with Buddhism. Even some Buddhist teachers say that Buddhism is not a religion, and I appreciate why some of them do this. It's one way to get people to see Buddhism as-it-is without trying to view it through an Abrahamic filter. Also, these days lots of people are so allergic to the R-word that as soon as they hear it, *they're outta there*. But I tend to agree with Karen Armstrong that saying Buddhism is not a religion is mostly western cultural bias.

Also, I hear from a lot of people that Buddhism is a philosophy, not a religion. While Buddhism doesn't fit into the standard western conceptual box marked "religion," if you get to know it well you understand Buddhism doesn't fit into the standard western conceptual box labeled "philosophy," either — unless you slice big chunks of it off first, which many do.

* * *

About God: There are infinite numbers of ways to understand God or gods, which I'll get into in a later chapter. For now I'll just say there is a vast and riotously diverse spectrum of understanding of God within monotheism. And when you wander outside of monotheism "god" can be understood so many different ways the word is almost meaningless.

In fact, not all religions have gods, exactly. Even some religions with gods may not consider relating to gods to be the ultimate concern of religion. In some of the traditions that emerged from Vedanta,[v] for example, the ultimate concern is not what sort of relationship one has with gods, however those "gods" are conceptualized. Rather, the ultimate concern is the absolute nature of existence and whether the self is or is not distinctively separate from everything else, including gods. (Answers vary.)

In a few religions (e.g., Jainism, Buddhism) gods may (or may not) pop up in the literature, but their role is auxiliary rather than central. In some circumstances they serve useful roles as archetypes, but outside of that it's okay to ignore them.

And I say — so much for the dictionary definitions of "religion" as being about worshiping gods.

I argue that the western conceptual box labeled "religion" has gotten so small and tight that little of the Wide World of Religion fits into it without considerable distortion. Even some of the more progressive factions within the Abrahamic religions get left out of it sometimes. Since the way we organize and classify information in our heads can either limit or enhance our ability to understand it, this is where we must start to rethink religion.

So let's talk about making the conceptual box bigger.

* * *

The word *religion* is from the Latin *religio*. However, the Romans did not agree among themselves what the word meant.

Cicero connected *religio* to *relegere*, which means to re-read or review a text, especially in a diligent manner. But other possible source words are *religare*, meaning to fasten or bind; *re-eligere*, meaning to "choose again," or *re-ligare,* meaning to bind back or re-connect. I'm partial to that last one.

I've also seen arguments that *religion* is from the Latin word for rules or ruling, either in the sense of regulation or sovereignty, but there doesn't seem to be much scholarly support for that view.

The "binding" or "binding back" definitions might make religion something akin to *yoga,* a Sanskrit word often translated as "discipline" that more literally means "union." The English *yoke* evolved from *yoga,* by the way. There are all kinds of yogas, many of which do *not* involve bending one's body into improbable positions.

If religion, at its root, is about union or re-connection, the next question is — union with *what?* Reconnection with *what?* Not all religious traditions will answer that question the same way.

For that matter, who is this person seeking union? What is the self? We all like to think we know who we are, but hardly any of us do. From birth we've been conditioned to understand ourselves as our families and culture define us, and we march through our lives conforming to our conditioning and measuring our value by our jobs and possessions.

But rip away our contexts, our connections, our *stuff,* and who are we, then? What's left?

One of religion's most ancient functions is to provide a means to step outside of our conditioning and connect to something beyond the limited self. That *something* may be God, although not necessarily. And in doing this, we may achieve a profoundly different understanding of ourselves.

Consider the story from the Chandogya Upanishad, in which a father, Uddalaka, helps his son Svetaketu perceive the vast, unlimited absolute reality beyond ordinary appearance. And then Uddalaka says, *tat tvam asi* — *thou art that.* Or, it's all you.

The physicist Erwin Schrödinger — yes, the Schrödinger of Schrödinger's cat — said of this,

> This life of yours which you are living is not merely a piece of this entire existence, but in a certain sense the whole; only this whole is not so constituted that it can be surveyed in one single glance. This, as we know, is what the Brahmins express in that sacred, mystic formula which is yet really so simple and so clear; *tat tvam asi,* this is you.

The familiar story of the Garden of Eden is the foundational myth of much of western religion. Understood literally, it's a stupid, pointless story. In the context of *mythos*, however, it is a rich allegory that speaks to us of exile or estrangement — from God, perhaps, or from nature, or from each other, or maybe even from ourselves. It can be understood many different ways.

This great myth poses questions to us, even today: Who are we? What are we missing? How do we reconnect?

* * *

A creed gives expression to a definite collective belief, whereas the word *religion* expresses a subjective relationship to certain metaphysical, extramundane factors. A creed is a confession of faith intended chiefly for the world at large and is thus an intramundane affair, while the meaning and purpose of religion lie in the relationship of the individual to God (Christianity, Judaism, Islam) or to the path of salvation and liberation (Buddhism). — [Carl Jung, *The Undiscovered Self* (1957)]

* * *

My working definition of *religion* is that it's a discipline or practice — not just a belief system — that enables one to experience, be at one with, or otherwise re-connect to an intangible *something* greater than the limited self. The something might be God, although not necessarily. The practice might involve prayer and worship, although not necessarily. And, yes, the discipline or practice probably is *framed* by doctrine that cannot be verified objectively but which might be personally verified in one way or another. But merely believing in the doctrine is not the point.

Some of you may think this is maddeningly vague. I acknowledge there may be holes in this definition, and so I invite and encourage further discussion. But this definition is one that takes in *all* of the world's spiritual traditions, not just the more conservative parts of the Big Three of Monotheism.

The critical point is that we're talking about experience and perception more than belief or intellectual knowledge. I think the *discipline* or *diligence* connotations are important, also. Passively believing a bunch of nonsense because you've been told you're supposed to believe it doesn't count as religion in my book (which this is).

Although there is considerable overlap, the distinction between religion and philosophy is that philosophy is primarily intellectual. Philosophy involves logic, critical analysis, and a search for explanation.

Religion (as I am defining it) is primarily perceptual and involves how one realizes, relates to, manifests or experiences (fill in the blank: one's soul, existence itself, the cosmos, God, absolute reality, the Great Ineffable Whatever). Actualizing a religion's teachings in the world in some way — through service or charity, for example — is part of this.

Religions usually do have a philosophical basis, of course, and come with some kind of doctrinal container that gives the perceptual experience some context. And many philosophies touch on religious matters. They're both about constructing meaning, although in a different way. As I said, there is considerable overlap.

There is also considerable overlap between religion and psychology. This may be more obvious in eastern religions than western ones, but I think it's true of western religion as well.

For example, some scholars say myths amounted to early forms of psychiatry. Karen Armstrong wrote,

> When a myth described heroes threading their way through labyrinths, descending into the underworld, or fighting monsters, these were not understood as primarily factual stories. They were designed to help people negotiate the obscure regions of the psyche, which are difficult to access but which profoundly influence our thought and behavior. People had to enter the warren of their own mind and fight their personal demons. When Freud and Jung began to chart their scientific search for the soul, they instinctively turned to these ancient myths. A myth was never intended as an accurate account of a historical event; it was *something that had in some sense happened once but that also happens all the time*. [Karen Armstrong, *The Case for God* (Random House, 2009), emphasis original]

A recurring theme in Armstrong's work is that the reason much contemporary religion is so sick and twisted is that it's trying to render *mythos* into an approximation of scientific reason, and *it doesn't work*. And trying to make it work has led a large part of our population into a dogmatic Twilight Zone.

* * *

Lest you think Christians will never agree to this, I say they already have. The notion that Christianity is mostly about arranging one's mental furniture in accord with a belief system would have been alien to most of the great Christian theologians of history. "Faith" to early Christian theologians — and many recent ones, for that matter — was not at all a synonym for belief. It was more about love of or trust in a God whose nature and opinions were beyond human understanding. To declare you know what God thinks about anything, including which politicians he supports, would have been blasphemy to them.

Another aspect of rethinking religion is rethinking religion *vis à vis* science. Science and religion have had a rocky relationship since the Renaissance and parted company entirely in the 19th century. They have yet to publicly reconcile, although in one way or another many individuals have reconciled science and religion for themselves.

I say the biggest barrier to this reconciliation is scriptural literalism, which I address in several places in this book. But the basic challenge to literalist religion is this: What is your religion *for*? Is it to teach us facts about biology, earth science and astrophysics? Or is it to guide us in our experience of living and dying?

Or, if that last bit doesn't jibe with the basic message of your religion, what does? Conservative Christians, for example, might want to think *really hard* whether denying science has anything whatsoever to do with what Jesus actually taught. And if not, why are they so opposed to science?

I suspect the honest answer to that question may have little to do with religion.

Let me be clear that I'm not talking about tearing down or merging together the established religious traditions. Each of the world's great religions has within it — somewhere in its foundational teachings and the written commentaries of its revered teachers and scholars — all of the elements it needs to be a positive and peaceful force, in individual lives and in the world. The challenge to religious people today is to bring these often overlooked parts of our respective heritages into a brighter light and make them a more visible part of our lives.

Although let's leave out the proselytizing, please? And we must stop letting the fundamentalists and literalists set all the rules and hog all the microphones.

* * *

In conclusion:

Let's get over the idea that religion is mostly about believing things. In many religious traditions beliefs are a vehicle, not a destination. In some religious traditions beliefs aren't even the vehicle, but more like training wheels.

And let us agree that religion is best regarded as a personal commitment and not something that entire societies must be cajoled or intimidated into accepting.

Other proposals to be explored in this book:

Religion can be a strategy for avoiding yourself, or it can be a means to come home to yourself.

Religion is as much about the intimate experience of the self as it is about celestial metaphysics. Maybe more so, sometimes.

Religion has physical as well as mental components; it is not something you do only inside your head.

Religion is a living process, and it will mature as you mature. If you are 50 and your religion is the same to you now that it was when you were 20, you're not doing it right.

3   Spiritual Is Religious

The Dao that can be talked about is not the Dao. — Dao De
Jing

Increasing numbers of people call themselves "spiritual but not religious."
Most people who say this seem to assume that "religious" means belong-
ing to an organized religion and "spiritual" is a do-it-yourself project.

Another way to understand the alleged distinction between "religious" and "spiritual" popped up in a paper published in 2012 in the journal *Social Psychological and Personality Science*. The authors — Jacob Hirsh,
Megan Walberg, and Jordan Peterson of the University of Toronto — determined that political conservatives tend to be *religious,* meaning they
place great importance on church attendance and the authority of established religious institutions. Liberals are *spiritual,* meaning they value feeling deeply connected to the universe.

For the record — *spiritual* is from the Latin *spiritus,* which refers to
breath and life. Early Christians were the first to use *spiritus* to mean
"soul." The use of *spirit* to refer to ghosts or other supernatural beings began in the 14th century.

To someone who has some knowledge of world religions and religious history, this divergence of *spiritual* and *religious* seems odd. As I just
argued in the previous chapter, one of the traditional basic functions of
many religions is to facilitate a connection to or union with something beyond the limited self, which could include the universe. So what's going
on here?

I propose that "spiritual but not religious" is largely a response to
the degradation of mythos in much established religion, as well as the ac-
companying rise in literalism that makes much established religion look
stupid. Some of us have spiritual longings that supernatural belief systems
just don't satisfy.

Further, for some people it's not enough to read a passage from an
old book saying that God loves them. They long for something that can be
experienced and, even better, could be *transformative.* And many spirituality
movements have sprung up that promise to provide this.

This movement away from "religion" and toward "spirituality" is, then, perfectly understandable. I also think it's a really bad idea.

Before I go any further, here's a disclaimer: The spirituality movement is varied and decentralized, and any generalizations one might make about it will not be true of all of it. Also, some years ago I also went through about a decade-long phase of being "unchurched" — wanting a spiritual home but not knowing where to find one — and I respect that spiritual seekers need time to check out whatever's *out there*. And at the moment, "spiritual but not religious" is what's out there. However ...

Putting aside the fact that much of the spiritual-but-not-religious movement appears to be about selling spirituality-related products (retreats, seminars, crystals, various decorative items, DVDs, natural and holistic remedies, jewelry, and, yes, books), much of it also seems palliative rather than curative. By that I mean big parts of it appear to be disinterested in connection with something beyond the limited self. Often the spirituality movement seems more about staying stuck in the limited self but feeling better about it.

This is a delicate point, and I hope to be clear here — ultimately, there are no "shoulds." We don't all have to follow the same set of rules about this religion/spirituality thing. I do advise choosing a path or practice because it resonates with you on a deep and intimate level, and not because someone recommended it or because the book about it is on the best-seller list. Whatever it is, the practice *should* "feel" right to you. I've heard many people say that when they finally found their spiritual tradition, even if it was very different from anything they'd experienced before, it felt like coming home.

But when we give ourselves permission to pick and choose from the spirituality buffet, most of us are going to choose things that feel comfortable rather than challenging, that confirm our existing worldview and reflect back to us the understanding we already have (or an idealized version of it), and that will enhance the person we think we are. This easily can become an exercise in reinforcing the ego rather than transcending it.

It also strikes me that even the better spiritual-but-not-religious authors and lecturers come up short in the *how-do-we-do-this* department. They're good at presenting a compelling perspective, but often they are hazy about how this perspective may be realized except in a conceptual way. Adjust your thinking all you like, but all the junk in your subconscious that is *really* jerking you around probably will remain untouched.

I'm not letting religion off the hook here. As I've already said, much of organized religion is a mess. The degradation of mythos and the rise of literalism has given us ghastly things, such as Pat Robertson saying that he knows global warming is a scam because there are no SUVs on Jupiter.[vi] Well, Pat Robertson generally.

Carl Jung wrote in *The Undiscovered Self*, "The Churches stand for traditional and collective convictions which in the case of many of their adherents are no longer based on their own inner experience but on *unreflecting belief*, which is notoriously apt to disappear as soon as one begins to think about it." Or else, one chooses to not think about it and instead clings to it more and more fanatically.

Often, even the less demented forms of contemporary religion not only lack a path of practice, they aren't even very good at the compelling perspective. An incomprehensible God one is supposed to believe in and pray to, *because*, can't always compete with many of the feel-good-about-yourself sales pitches of nontraditional spirituality.

I suspect this failure to provide a compelling perspective is at least partly behind the slow decline in membership of the mainline Protestant denominations. This decline is unfortunate, because many of these denominations are more progressive, less literalist, and more in touch with science and scholarly theology than the 700 Club version of Christianity. For example, 78 percent of U.S. white mainline Protestants accept human evolution as fact, as compared to 27 percent of white Evangelicals and 76 percent of the religiously unaffiliated, according to a Pew survey published in December 2013.[vii]

I've read that most of the people who drift away from one of these denominations don't choose another religious tradition or atheism. For the most part they still believe in God, but they remain unchurched. It appears that once social convention no longer demanded that everyone dress up and go to church on Sunday morning, many people stopped going. Singing some old hymns and listening to a sermon just wasn't compelling to them. Instead of offering a path toward something beyond the limited self; traditional Protestantism often is more of an assurance that there *is* something beyond the limited self, but you'll just have to take our word for it. And don't miss our next potluck supper.

And I suspect increasing numbers of young people stay away from religion because they see the whackjobs — excuse me, religious people — on television, and hear them ranting against sex, scientific advancement, Harry Potter, tolerance of others' differences and most of the other things that make life nice, and they think *that's what all religion is like*. Just check out comments on any spirituality (but not religion) forum some time. I honestly think many of the young folks don't understand that not all organized religion is fundamentalism.

* * *

Oh, you can get an *experience* in some churches, certainly. I grew up in the Ozark Mountain section of the Bible Belt, also called the Land of Perpetual Holy Spirit Gospel Tabernacle Revivals. Once I encountered a boy with a cast on his leg who told me he had broken it in church. How so? He had been filled with the Spirit, he said, and had tried to jump over the pews.

I was raised Lutheran, so my personal memories of church are not nearly so *vivid*.

Yes, it's exhilarating to be part of a group having a big, rowdy, cathartic experience, That's why people like to watch big sporting events like the Super Bowl in groups, because if your team wins — *wow*. How much fun is that, right? Watching the same game by yourself just isn't the same experience.

At their peak, such experiences can give you a temporary sense of being liberated from yourself, as some part of your identity forgets itself amid the collective excitement. I've been talking about experience or perception beyond the limits of the self, and intense group experiences where everyone gets emotionally high together can give you a fleeting taste of that.

However, a church with rousing services may generate the high every time and attract a huge following, but without also allowing for personal reflection, contemplation and questioning, it's feeding the congregation spiritual junk food. You might be better off sticking to being a sports fan.

And I'm not saying that rousing church services are always bad. There's a time and place for them. A good Gospel choir can almost inspire me to re-convert, believe me. I'm just saying to be careful. There's a difference between an intimate experience of the Great Ineffable Whatever and *avoiding* an intimate experience of anything by submerging yourself into a group.

* * *

It's also the case that as congregations fall further down the rabbit hole of dogmatism and fundamentalism, or the more ministers resort to stoking fear of God and hellfire to keep the flock from going astray, the more those religions will inculcate a circle-the-wagons, us-against-the-world mentality that is not just psychologically unhealthy; it's also a cornerstone of religious violence. And it's taking religion in the opposite direction from feeling connected to the universe, or even God.

As much as conservative Christians extol the value of the "fear of God," I submit that the "fear of God" is psychologically twisted, even putting aside the question of whether there is a God or not (to be dealt with in the next chapter). If we define *faith* as trust or confidence in God, as many of the great Christian theologians defined it, then *fear* of God is the opposite of faith even in Christian terms.

A world experienced with and projected by fear is a word full of dangers and scary things, and the first priority for the fearful is self-protection. And the psychological walls go up, and the fearful become more and more cut off from genuine intimacy, with themselves and everyone else, and also cut off from the clear and direct experience of life, never mind God.

Fear is also a well-known gateway drug to fanaticism. Nothing good comes of that.

* * *

To decide that a certain teaching is worthwhile simply because it echoes our established opinion is very unwise. Along that easy course there is no new discovery of truth, only more stale habit. [Bhikkhu Nyanasobhano, *Available Truth: Excursions Into Buddhist Wisdom and the Natural World* (Wisdom Publications, 2007)]

* * *

And here's the point: I say that religion and spirituality need each other. It's a big mistake to separate them. Religion divorced from spirituality too easily becomes either social convention or a weird supernatural ideology. Spirituality without the grounding and direction of religious tradition too easily becomes just a self-improvement project at best, or at worst can be a self-indulgent fantasy or an endless, directionless search for the newest spiritual/emotional "fix."

So let's talk about reconciling spirituality and religion. How might that be done?

Rekindling an appreciation for mythos is a start, and I say this must be done to save religion, although that's not going to be easy. But religion does give us some tools to work with.

Going back millennia, a great many religions have used a variety of physical practices — e.g., rituals and sacraments, aestheticism, prayer, meditation, dancing, prostrations, chanting, singing, yoga, even martial arts — that ultimately were about connecting *somehow* to *something* on a not-conceptual level. The thing connected with could be God, or gods, or nature, or one's ancestors, or everything in the cosmos throughout space and time. The Great Ineffable Whatever.

Intimately experiencing the Great Ineffable Whatever is the *sine qua non* of many long-established religions. And yes, I'm talking about Buddhism here, but more than that I'm talking about *mysticism*.

And please don't run screaming from *mysticism*. It's a word; it won't jump off the page and bite you.

Once again, though, I must define terms. I see a lot of writers using *mysticism* as a synonym for *superstition*. It can mean that, in some contexts, but it also means a lot of other things.

The word *mysticism* evolved from the Greek *mystikos,* meaning secret or hidden. It originally referred to esoteric rituals and teachings.

In early Christianity, one form of mysticism was a practice of prying secret allegorical meanings out of scripture. Another presumed the presence of invisible things or beings, especially during sacraments. Understood this way, mysticism does appear to be about the supernatural.

By the Middle Ages, however, Christian mysticism was about having a direct experience of the divine. This experience was not an end in itself but rather a means of personal transcendence or transformation. And this is where spirituality comes in.

The Stanford Encyclopedia of Philosophy[viii] defines "mystical experience" as "A (purportedly) super sense-perceptual or sub sense-perceptual experience granting acquaintance of realities or states of affairs that are of a kind not accessible by way of sense perception, somatosensory modalities, or standard introspection."

I tripped over "somatosensory modalities," too. I think it refers to the sense of touch and other sensations of the body, but I'm not going to swear to that.

Anyway, in plain English, a mystical experience in this sense is one that is neither sensory nor conceptual. It is *not* dependent on seeing visions or hearing voices. It is not generated by reason or intellect.

Through this experience, one may feel an intimate connection of existence beyond self, or realize something about the nature of reality not perceived before.

The spiritual-but-not-religious crowd calls these *spiritual* experiences, but it's the same thing. Prominent atheist Sam Harris (author, neuroscientist, co-founder of Project Reason) has written quite a bit about spiritual experience, such as —

> There is no question that people have "spiritual" experiences (I use words like "spiritual" and "mystical" in scare quotes, because they come to us trailing a long tail of metaphysical debris). Every culture has produced people who have gone off into caves for months or years and discovered that certain deliberate uses of attention—introspection, meditation, prayer—can radically transform a person's moment to moment perception of the world. [ix]

—although Harris is determined to not connect these experiences to *religion* in any way, because of the "metaphysical debris." People might erroneously think they're having an experience of God or Brahman or some such, which is atheistically incorrect. Of course, God or Brahman can be understood in many different ways, to be discussed in the next chapter.

This realized thing may be outside conventional frames of reference but is not necessarily supernatural or contradictory to science. Often the experience defies description, possibly (and I'm guessing here) because it engages a level of awareness that doesn't primarily involve the brain's left temporal lobe. Or, perhaps language simply hasn't been devised to describe it. *The Dao that can be talked about is not the Dao.*

In the sense I am using it, mysticism is about engaging in practices designed to affect one's perceptions — for example, the perception of feeling deeply connected to the universe — in order to bring about some kind of personal transcendence, or change how we perceive ourselves and our lives, or to realize some understanding of or connection with the Great Ineffable Whatever.

My first Zen teacher, the late John Daido Loori Roshi, used to say that Zen is pure mysticism. In the case of Zen, the definition "direct experience of the divine" doesn't work, because Zen doesn't divide phenomena into "divine" and "not-divine" categories. But, ultimately, that's just a conceptual quibble, I think. Mystical experience *can* take you to a place where the conceptual quibbles no longer matter.

Over the centuries much of the once-thriving mystical traditions of Christianity faded away, along with mythos, and were replaced by religion-as-ideology. Humble appreciation for the deep mystery of existence was replaced with dogmatic certitude.

Among other effects — Christianity, the tradition of saints Augustine of Hippo and Francis of Assisi, was reduced to Jerry Falwell babbling that Tinky Winky the Teletubby was gay.

*   *   *

Mystics generally are not given to literal or dogmatic interpretations of scripture, because what is perceived in mystical practice often cannot be captured in words and concepts. This can make dogmatists crazy.

For example, mystical Islam is associated with the Sufi tradition, and today Islamic fundamentalists are targeting Sufi mosques. In recent years a number of Sufi mosques and shrines in Pakistan have been destroyed by suicide bombers and grenade-tossing Taliban followers. In Libya, ultra-conservative Islamists leveled a large Sufi mosque in the middle of Tripoli with a bulldozer, in broad daylight. Police not only didn't stop the destruction but, allegedly, took part.[x]

The great Christian mystics of the European Middle Ages left us some treasures of religious literature, sometimes written secretly while the dogmatists down the road were organizing crusades and running inquisitions. The Christian mystical traditions of Europe faded away after the 17th century or so, however, leaving the dogmatists pretty much alone on the field.

Back in the 1960s the Trappist monk and priest Thomas Merton began a personal exploration of mystical practices of Buddhism, including Zen meditation, called *zazen*. His purpose, I understand, was to find a way to re-ignite the Catholic mystical tradition. I've heard through Buddhist sources that right before his accidental death in 1968 Father Merton had arranged to study with a Tibetan Dzogchen master, which would have been interesting, as Dzogchen is *out there*. It's a shame the quest was cut short.

But to this day there are still some Catholic monks, nuns and priests who practice zazen, sitting in silence and stillness, opening themselves to a direct and intimate experience of the divine. I know this because I have met a few of them. Father Merton and his quest are not forgotten.

*   *   *

Offerings are made to the invisible powers, formidable blessings are pronounced, and all kinds of solemn rites are performed. Everywhere and at all times there have been *rites d'entrée et de sortie* whose magical efficacy is denied and which are impugned as magic and superstition by rationalists incapable of psychological insight. But magic has above all a psychological effect whose importance should not be underestimated. [Carl Jung, *The Undiscovered Self*]

* * *

If we don't live in monasteries, if we have jobs and families and commitments in the world, we may think this mysticism stuff won't work for us. But that's not entirely true.

Through human history, most of the world's religions functioned by combining various mystical or worshipful practices with whatever doctrine that tradition accepted as authentic. And through most of human history, the practices were emphasized more than the doctrines. In some times and places it wasn't considered important for laypeople to understand doctrines at all. For most people, in most of human history, religion was all about the rituals.

Ritual and modernity don't appear to get along, however. I've met people who are adamantly hostile to ever taking part in religious rituals, even if they are seeking some kind of spiritual experience. Unfortunately some of these people stumble into Zen centers and are dismayed to find out that Zen can be one ritual after another. The people who write Zen books don't always tell you that, but that's how it is. Sorry.

Let's talk about the purpose of religious ritual.

Often the stated purpose is to evoke the attention or presence of some invisible celestial being, which as I mentioned earlier is one of the older forms of mysticism. If you don't believe in invisible celestial beings, however, such rituals can seem stupid. I understand that.

However, there are other reasons.

Another way to think of ritual is that it's an activity to make something visible or tangible that before was invisible or intangible. Rites of passage are a good example. Rite of passage ceremonies are a way to publicly acknowledge that a person has achieved some sort of status change — he or she is now an adult, or married, or a high school graduate.

Of course, we can do that on Facebook now, but it's not the same thing.

We might think of a wedding ceremony as something that binds two people in marriage. But another way to think of it is that two people already are bound in love and commitment, and the ceremony just makes that commitment publicly visible and officially acknowledged. That's what I mean by making something visible that was invisible. The "something" is not necessarily supernatural.

Rituals and ceremonies can be a way for people to share or make tangible their joys and sorrows. Sometimes we humans have a deep psychological need to do this. Funerals can help people accept the death of a loved one, for example.

There is also the relatively recent phenomenon of spontaneous shrines popping up after a terrible tragedy, such as one of our frequent mass shootings. People bring flowers, cards, candles and sometimes toys to leave near the place where the terrible thing happened. They do this because it helps them process the sorrow they feel. Sharing an emotional burden with others in a physical, tangible way really can lighten it by helping us feel connected to each other.

* * *

I was in lower Manhattan on September 11, 2001, and was an eyewitness to the collapse of the World Trade Center towers.

Two days later I was back in Manhattan, and I played hooky from my job for a time to wander about the city. I was heartsick beyond description, and I needed to wander.

I walked 42nd Street from Grand Central toward Broadway. Lampposts were covered with fliers seeking missing loved ones, all bearing a photograph of a smiling man or woman we all already knew was gone. But hope is a hard thing to let go of.

I looked up Madison Avenue as I crossed, and American flags already were displayed in front of most of the buildings. In a few days Manhattan would be thoroughly saturated in stars and stripes.

Construction workers in Times Square had little American flags on stick flag posts attached to their helmets and messages of defiance flying from all the scaffolding.

From Times Square I took a downtown subway to Union Square. A middle-aged man seated near me in the subway car was talking to himself. He was well groomed and wore a good suit and a gold watch. He may have worked on Wall Street. And he was shaking, visibly. He talked to himself and trembled like a torn autumn leaf barely attached to the tree.

Other riders, very likely strangers to him, stood silently around him like protective, swaying angels. The concern for him was palpable.

In Union Square someone had left big roles of brown paper and markers, and people knelt on the pavement and grass around George Washington's statue and wrote their thoughts. By the time I got there, there were many yards of thoughts. I read them and was struck that most were expressions of hope or condolence, not vengeance. After one of the few wishes for vengeance, someone else had written, "An eye for an eye leaves the whole world blind." Not original, I know, but appropriate.

I love New York, and since that day I've loved New Yorkers.

In the next few days all of Manhattan turned into a spontaneous shrine. People left flowers and cards around the lampposts still bearing the fading "have you seen this person?" fliers. Written messages and flags covered block after block of street-level scaffolding. Wreaths and bouquets were piled in front of fire and police stations. A big open area in the Times Square subway station became a sea of flowers, cards, candles — sometimes lit — and mementos.

It was messy, as human life and grief and experience are messy. But it was a way for grieving people to reach out to each other, to confirm to each of us that we were not alone in our grief. And it really did help.

* * *

The communion ceremony is among the most solemn observances of Christianity. It is not understood or practiced in the same way in all denominations, however. In some the bread and wine *are* the body and blood of Christ, who is understood to be present. In others the ceremony is an act of remembrance and reflection.

I'm going to skip discussion of how ceremonies and sacraments are explained in doctrine and instead talk about how ceremonies, sacraments, rites and rituals are *experienced*. I do not mean to imply that how a ceremony is understood, how it is framed by doctrine, is unimportant. Of course, it is very important. But this is something the myriad religious traditions have to work out for themselves. As we'd say back home in the Ozarks, I don't have a dog in that hunt.

Old-style communion involves approaching the altar (usually with a group, pew by pew), bowing or kneeling, having a wafer placed on one's tongue, and then sipping wine from a common chalice held by the priest or pastor. This was how things were done in my church-of-origin in which I was confirmed, way back when. The ceremony requires paying some attention to what you are doing, at least so you don't trip or drop the wafer or drool the wine. It was also something the whole congregation did, physically, together.

In some of my friends' Evangelical churches, the practice was to keep people in their seats and instead pass trays of whatever bread product they used and other trays bearing little glasses of grape juice. God doesn't approve of alcohol, apparently, so the "wine" referenced in the Gospels is the one biblical fact that isn't literal. Still, it was all solemn and taken very seriously.

Once, out of curiosity, I tried to find out if some version of communion is observed in those big megachurches one reads about. I'm still not sure about all of them. But in at least one, I have read, the ushers pass out cardboard, shrink-wrapped kits containing one wafer and a little plastic container of grape juice. I don't know if the ushers collect the trash or if people toss it into big trash bins on their way to the parking lot.

I confess that this bothers me. Reverence for the objects used in ritual is a nearly universal feature of religious observance, so the disposable kits are a huge break from traditional standards. Still, unless we assume ritual objects have magic powers — and I don't say they do — why does it matter?

Across religious traditions, ceremonies and rituals function to create a sanctified space, and those who enter that space are dedicating themselves to fulfillment of the ultimate concern of their religion, whatever that is. The space is sanctified by the participants' own reverence and devotion, and ritual objects such as chalices, crosses, incense and candles give physical presence to that reverence and devotion.

The disposable kits may be practical, but it seems to me they turn Christ into McJesus — just another consumer product.

At another megachurch, I'm told, the bread and grape juice are set up buffet-style to one side, and people are encouraged to consume said bread and grape juice at their convenience. This doesn't even qualify as a ceremony, I don't think.

Again, I'm not saying that rituals and ritual objects have magic power. I'm saying that rituals and ceremonies, when carried out with care and attention, can have a palpable psychological impact on the participants that really can expand awareness and change perspectives.

Put another way, the value of ceremonies and rituals isn't determined by consuming the "right" spiritual product. There is nothing magical about eating a wafer or slurping a beverage even assuming somebody prayed over these consumables before they were arranged on the buffet table. Instead, the value of a ceremony or ritual is found in the *experience* of it.

I came to appreciate this from Zen. I've already said Zen can be one ritual after another. For example, upon entering a Zen meditation or ceremonial hall, one keeps silence. There are rules for which foot you place inside the threshold first. One's hands are supposed to be folded in a particular manner. There are bowing protocols for taking one's seat. And so on.

These rituals annoy the stuffing out of a lot of people, who assume this is all *beyond anal*. Sometimes it is. But the first thing the rituals do is cause you to *pay attention*, to be mindful. You are mindful of your hands, the sensation of your bare feet touching the floor, the candles on the altar, the other people already seated. You train yourself to be completely present, mentally and physically, as are the other people in the hall. In the silence and stillness, you are all completely present together.

It gets intense.

This is hard to explain to someone who hasn't experienced it for himself, but ritual, if carried out mindfully, *can* bring the mythos and teaching of a religious tradition "into the body" (as we say in Zen) or into one's awareness in a way that is not intellectual or conceptual. This engages personal experience on a very intimate level. Consciousness expands; the unfathomable mysteries of life and death, time and being, become immanent.

I doubt this will happen when the "ritual" resembles getting fast food at a drive-through, however.

Mindfulness has become such a fad lately I wish I could avoid the word. I'm not sure everyone who talks about mindfulness means the same thing by it. Done correctly, however, it really can quiet the distracting chatter in our heads and enhance our awareness of the present moment. In time an individual may become more aware of the intuitive and emotional processes that social psychologists tell us are really forming our opinions and making our decisions. This in turn can change how we understand many things, including ourselves.

I suspect that at least some of the resistance among spiritual seekers to taking part in rituals springs from a deep-down fear of intimacy. But self-intimacy is essential to the spiritual path. Chasing spiritual "enlightenment" or a connection to God while avoiding yourself is something like trying to learn to swim while avoiding water.

*   *   *

For see, thou wast within and I was without, and I sought thee out there. Unlovely, I rushed heedlessly among the lovely things thou hast made. Thou wast with me, but I was not with thee. These things kept me far from thee; even though they were not at all unless they were in thee. [Saint Augustine of Hippo, *Confessions*]

* * *

One more Zen story — I genuinely love this stuff — there's a text of Soto Zen called the "Tenzo kyokun,"[xi] or "Instructions for the Cook," written by the 13th century Japanese master Eihei Dogen. This text is exactly what the title says — job instructions for a chief cook of a monastery, an honored position usually given to a senior monk regardless of cooking ability.

For Dogen, cooking was a kind of ritual. Cooking, and everything else in daily life, was an opportunity for waking up. He advised the cook to handle pots and spoons with reverence and treat each grain of rice with as much care and attention as if it were his own eyeball. Then he said,

Taking up a vegetable leaf manifests the Buddha's sixteen-foot golden body; take up the sixteen-foot golden body and reveal it as a vegetable leaf. This is the power of functioning freely as the awakening activity that benefits all beings.

The sanctified space reaches everywhere. And bleep the cardboard, shrink-wrapped, disposable communion kits.

* * *

I've been a Zen student — not always a diligent one — for more than a couple of decades. A story I've heard from others many times is that the very thing about Zen they thought was most boring or annoying — bowing, chanting, whatever —was what they were doing the first time they experienced *kensho,* which means "seeing one's true nature." Kensho is an initial experience of direct insight or awakening that can be significant to one's spiritual journey.

And the moral is that until it happens you can't possibly know what's going to work for you, what's going to open the perceptual door. If you are a true spiritual seeker, you must always be ready to go somewhere you didn't expect to go.

This is why a lot of us working to establish Buddhism in the West are reluctant to toss out all the rituals, even though others accuse us of being anal or just slavishly mimicking Asian practices. It's understood in Zen that the value of a ritual does not lie in whether some unseen spirit is present, but in the psychological impact the ritual has on participants. When the ritual is carried out with great care and focus, and all participants are fully present, that impact can be palpable. I'm sure this also is true if you are lighting Shabbat candles, singing a Sikh hymn, or offering incense to Ganesha.

I urge both spiritual seekers and clergy to reconsider the role of ceremonies and rituals and whether we've gone too far in de-ritualizing our religious observances. And if you're doing a ceremony, do a ceremony. Be focused. Be reverent. Pay attention to all the details. People who don't have an active role should be quiet and just be entirely *there*. Don't worry if what you're doing makes conceptual sense, because that's not what it's for. Don't be afraid of silence; you don't *have* to have organ music oozing away in the background all the time. Give silence a try, anyway. The fewer the sensory distractions, the greater the intimacy.

Music has its place, though. I love to sing and over the years have taken part in performances of much of the western sacred music repertoire as well a few operas. Once in a great while, when everyone is fully present and *in* the music, an ecstatic presence takes hold of the singers and musicians that I can't quite describe, but it's not just an emotional high. The Welsh call this *hwyl*, but I've never seen an English translation of hwyl that does the word justice.

I wrote earlier of the slow loss of membership among mainline Protestant Churches. Some of these denominations downplay ritual and mystery, and that may be part of the problem. This approach may make God may seem more theoretical than immanent.

In her book *The Case for God*, Karen Armstrong recalled examples of gods in early religions who became too lofty, too removed from human life. "Reduced to a mere explanation — to what would later be called the First Cause or Prime Mover — he became *Deus otiosus*; a 'useless' or 'superfluous' deity, and gradually faded from the consciousness of his people…. No god can survive unless he or she is actualized by the practical activity of ritual."

* * *

One more note on rituals — I understand that some recent psychological studies have found a correlation between regular church/mosque/temple attendance and an increased tendency toward religious tribalism and violence toward those outside the tribe. These studies sometimes name ritual as being the bonding agent that creates an in group/out group perception.

I'm a bit at a loss to answer this, because the studies are all behind firewalls and I only know what I read *about* them. At least one study seems to equate attendance at a religious service with "ritual," and I dispute that; one is not necessarily the other. As I've already illustrated, chopping carrots or cooking a pot of rice can be more of a genuine religious ritual than church attendance.

It's also the case, according to the study I cited at the beginning of this chapter, that conservatives tend to place greater value than liberals on the authority of religious institutions. So we may be looking at a population that was predisposed toward greater mistrust of the "other" even without ritual.

However, these studies also could be showing us something about the psychological power of ritual, and that this power is to be used carefully. I propose that ritual *per se* is neither harmful nor helpful, but perhaps it's how the participants understand and relate to the ritual that makes the difference.

* * *

I appreciate that there is a mistrust of mysticism among both the religious and non-religious. Like spirituality generally, if it's not guided or grounded by an established path of practice it can get weird and become just a projection of our own craziness. For this reason, do-it-yourself mysticism is a really bad idea.

Whether we want to admit it or not, our brains and nervous systems are not exactly cool, precise machines. It's closer to the truth to think of them as an oozy mess of delusions and biases under the direction of an ego whose primary job is to protect itself. As part of that job, most egos are very good at seeing what they want to see while editing out what they don't want to see, "real" or not. Realities that don't conform to our pre-set models are re-shaped in our heads so that they do. Something entirely outside our usual frames of reference may not make it through our cognitive filters at all; instead, our senses and brains will render it into something entirely different from what it really is.

Put another way, we're all lost in a fog of our own projections. Many great spiritual teachers have been saying this for millennia, and current research in psychology and neuroscience appears to confirm it. That being so, how can we guide ourselves? How do we trust our own experiences? And, make no mistake; ultimately we must trust our own experiences. Not trusting our own experiences is not psychologically healthy, I don't think.

Religions have answered this question in different ways. Dogmatic religions just hand you a preset belief system and say, *here, trust this. This is reality. Pay no attention to anything else.* If you are spiritual but not religious, it may be because you saw no compelling reason to trust that. Yeah, me neither.

The flip side of dogmatism might be called guru-ism, or unquestioning devotion to a particular teacher in the belief that he or she has all the answers and can fix whatever is wrong with you, somehow. But no human being has all the answers, and no human being can fix you but you. That's the truth of it.

Self-intimacy and trust — trust in yourself and in however you understand the Great Ineffable Whatever — are two essential components of the spiritual path. I advise avoiding any religious tradition that discourages self-intimacy and trust in favor of loyalty to group and dogma and dependency on whoever's in charge. However, there really are religious traditions that provide guidance, mentoring and support for developing self-intimacy and trust.

Where you go from here is up to you, but if you are a spiritual/religious sort of person I advise finding some middle way between ego-directed and other-directed spirituality. At times you may have to walk that lonesome valley by yourself, but it's good to have a map and a flashlight, and maybe someone to call when you are particularly lost.

* * *

People who turn to religion as adults usually do so because they are really unhappy or in some kind of crisis. And this makes them vulnerable. They will frantically grab at anything that gives them some hope or assurance, like a drowning man grabbing at a life buoy, but the thing grabbed at may cause them to sink instead of float.

Especially if you are in an anxious or excitable state of mind, your brain will arrange for you to see what you want to see — the face of Jesus imposed on your toasted cheese sandwich, for example — and hear what you want to hear. This is very common.

You might be surprised how easy it is to hallucinate, and not just when your emotions are in overdrive. Your senses and nervous system are designed to stay busy. Along with over-excitement, any kind of sensory deprivation also can cause your senses to manufacture things for themselves to do, and as a result you may see, hear, or feel things that bear no connection to external stimuli.

This is not unusual during long meditation retreats, for example. Usually this doesn't "mean" anything. It's just your nervous system misfiring. However, if you've been meditating for twelve hours a day for five days straight, you may welcome the diversion.

I do not discount the possibility that a particular dream or inexplicable sensory experience may be trying to tell you something that requires attention. I tend to think such things originate in the subconscious, not from invisible beings "out there" somewhere. And I also think sometimes our subconscious "knows" things our rational mind doesn't. As a rule of thumb, however, visions or other inexplicable events, especially those that show you what you want to see and confirm what you already believe, are just your own projections. Don't attach any importance to them. If they keep happening, through, do see a neurologist.

There's an old Zen story commonly told to beginners — once a new monk ran to his teacher and said, "Roshi! I was meditating in my room just now, and I saw the Buddha!"

"Well, don't let him bother you," the Roshi said. "Just keep meditating, and he'll go away."

* * *

A Memory: When Daido Loori (he wasn't called "Roshi" yet) officially became abbot of the Buddhist monastery he founded (Zen Mountain Monastery in Mt. Tremper, New York), the monastery held a big whoop-dee-doo observance called the Mountain Seat Ceremony. This was attended by prominent Zen teachers from across America as well as some local Christian clergy, the Karma Kagyu Tibetan monks from up the road and two busloads of Soto Zen monks and a couple of nuns from Japan.

But the interesting part for this discussion is that at one point, Daido Loori offered incense to Jesus and to the 16th-century Catholic mystic Saint Teresa of Avila, recognizing them as spiritual ancestors along with many masters from Asian Buddhist history. I don't recall that anyone at the ceremony thought that was odd.

* * *

Although I am stressing the commonalities of religious experience, I am not arguing for throwing out all the doctrines and making one big happy peace, love and brotherhood religion.

Part of the mystery that is religion is that it's not the commonalities but the distinctions that give the various traditions their particular transformative powers. The transformative power of Christianity lies in faith in the redemptive power of Jesus. The transformative power of Islam lies in surrendering one's will to Allah. The transformative power of Buddhism lies in direct insight into the illusory nature of the self. And so on. If you mush them all together, that's what you end up with — mush. If you're a spiritual seeker, my advice is to pick a tradition that resonates with you, and follow it.

If religious institutions give you the willies, which I understand: Although "tradition" and "institution" usually live under the same roof, they are not necessarily the same thing. It's entirely possible to practice within a religious *tradition* while maintaining an objective and even critical perspective of the *institution* that "contains" it. I recommend this, in fact.

Following a tradition is not what a lot of spiritual seekers want to hear. They want to hear that they don't need priests or gurus or teachers; they don't need a bunch of old doctrines; they can find God (or Whatever) themselves, thank you.

That sounds grand, but there's something missing — namely, *how do you do it?* How do you achieve this great connection so that it's real and not a projection of your own ego? Be advised: When your spiritual guide is your own ego, you're in trouble. Egos are the worst liars in the cosmos.

I acknowledge that some teachers and clergy with proper institutional "cred" can be jerks and charlatans and even predators. Never check your brain at the door. But the advantage of a long-established tradition is that, over the centuries, people who have gone before have marked the road and put traffic cones around the potholes, so to speak.

4 God and Existence

God is a metaphor for that which transcends all levels of intellectual thought. It's as simple as that. — Joseph Campbell

Not everybody agrees with Joseph Campbell that God is a metaphor, but a
lot of very religious people do agree. I've talked to them myself. And this
includes *God-believing* religious people.

Whatever you believe, for now, let's pretend that Campbell was
right, and God is a metaphor. A metaphor for what, however? If you lined
up 50 religious people and asked them to explain what God represents,
metaphorically, you might get 50 different answers. God isn't any one
thing to everybody. To different people, God could be anything from a
cosmic super-being, to a kind of universal intelligence residing outside
normal time and space, to the ground of being or the absolute basis of existence.

An actual Christian theologian named Paul Tillich is credited with
the "God is the ground of being" idea, although it can be traced back to
other theologians who lived centuries ago. These days on web discussion
forums, Tillich often is cited in "oh, yeah?" retorts to both stuck-in-the-
mud literalists and derisive atheists. He's probably never been so popular.

If God is the ground of being, maybe God is the Dharmadatu,
which in Buddhism is a field of limitless, all-pervading space in which all
phenomena take form, abide, and cease. It's something like the Higgs
Field, I think.

The point is that God isn't any one thing to everybody. Not everyone who believes in God believes in an anthropomorphic super-being who
hates homosexuals and takes sides in team competitions. Understanding of
"God" is so varied, in fact, that I say the word "God" has no specific, intrinsic meaning, and that it can be understood only within context.

So, atheists, will you please stop making fun of God by calling him
a "sky fairy"? It's ignorant. I don't believe in the Abrahamic God, either,
and I still think it's ignorant.

That said, it's also true that some, if not most, believers treat God
as a blank slate on which to project their deepest longings for something to
relieve their existential angst. This projection is often of a fatherly figure

who will protect them from scary things like death and generally be, well, fatherly.

To much of today's political-religious Right, "God" obviously is a collaboration of many projections, an amorphous collective fantasy that perfectly reflects and confirms their fears, biases, resentments, and various social and psychological pathologies.

However, just because people treat God as a cosmic projection screen doesn't prove there *isn't* one. It just tells us that we can't imagine what God is, so we fill in the blanks with what we want God to be.

Humans have a persistent tendency to imagine things we can't comprehend. Our brains are wired to do that, I suspect. So whenever we're confronted with something we can't comprehend, our brains will render it into something comprehendible. When we non-physicists hear about things like black holes or quarks, for example, usually our brain will do its best to form an image or impression to go with the name. "Quark" calls up for me the image of a little sparkly star bouncing around like a ping-pong ball on meth. I assume real quarks are not like that.

The point is that our tendency to mis-imagine things is not proof that the thing we mis-imagine doesn't exist. And just because people tend to imagine God as being something like a man — God made in man's image — is not proof there is no God.

I'm not actually arguing *for* the existence of God, mind you; I'm just saying that unless we all agree what God is — and we don't — God's existence is something that arguments can neither prove nor disprove, and it's futile and stupid to try.

*   *   *

Arguments about the existence of God, either for or against, always strike me as a desperate grasping at metaphysical straws. And such arguments in popular media usually are doubly stupid, because both sides invariably are arguing over the most banal and infantile God projections humanity has contrived.

There's a deliciously snarky book titled *Dispirited: How Contemporary Spirituality Makes Us Stupid, Selfish and Unhappy* by David Webster, an atheist who teaches a course in religion, philosophy and ethics at the University of Gloucester (UK). I only agree with about half of what Webster wrote in the book, and where I disagree with him I disagree with him *a lot*, but the book was still a fun read.

Anyway, Webster has some words for both the crusading atheists "Dawkins, Dennett, et al." and the defenders of whatever definition of God they're defending —

> "I want to suggest here that this debate has become ever more futile, distracting, and shrill. . . . Further, both sides are ever-more prone to treating religious faith merely as a matter of correspondence-theory metaphysics. Colleagues will know, and readers can surmise in safety, that I am not the world's biggest fan of Theology — but it's as if the discipline has never existed. You'd never know that reflective, intelligent, humane and critical people had actually given the nature and content of religion some sustained and rigorous inspection already." [David Webster, *Dispirited* (Zero Books, 2012)]

There's no question a lot of God-concepts and many common religious beliefs are silly, but other God-concepts are subtle and sophisticated enough to compete with quantum physics, at least on the scale of how smart you have to be to comprehend them. I wouldn't mind the crusading atheists' attacks on the low-hanging fruit of entrenched dogmatism and literalism, which I don't like, either. But when they frame today's clown-shoes version of popular religiosity as the entirety of religion — completely ignoring *millennia* of exegesis and commentaries and the protestations of living religious people who say their understanding of God is something else entirely — they're being willfully bigoted and ignorant themselves.

* * *

After immersing myself in an Asian tradition for a number of years, I came to realize that the way Asian religions conceptualize "God" or "gods" often is radically different from the way westerners conceptualize gods. Various characters from Asian art and literature get called "gods" because we don't have another word for them in English, but calling them "gods" often is unhelpful to understanding what they actually represent in their traditions.

For example, although Buddhists often say Buddhism isn't about gods, in Buddhist art and scriptures there are three basic kinds of characters often identified as gods. One kind are the *devas*, beings who live in the deva realms of old Buddhist cosmology. I'm told *deva* is Sanskrit for "being of light" or "shining one," and the word often is translated "god," although it might refer to any exalted person. Devas pop up in a lot of the sutras, and often casual observers of Buddhism seize upon the devas and say, ah-HAH! There *are* gods in Buddhism.

About the devas: Early Buddhists not only believed in a flat earth, but also in a flat cosmos with several layers. This cosmos was divided into three "worlds" with 31 "realms," one of which was the realm of humans.[xii] There were a number of heavenly deva realms, and some devas were enlightened beings while others were just oblivious. I'm not going to swear on a stack of sutras that *nobody* believes in this literally any more, but the 31 realms have been widely accepted as allegorical by many Buddhists for some time.

The important point about devas is that *they don't do anything for humans that gods normally do*. They are characters in stories who have their own problems. They don't control the weather or harvests or fertility or do anything useful or practical. They rarely have anything to do with humans and the human realm. Even if they were "real," there is nothing to be gained by worshipping or praying to them. You can be an entirely devout, practicing Buddhist and ignore them.

Tantric deities make up the second group, and these are a little harder to explain. Buddhist tantra is associated with the Tibetan schools and also with a Japanese sect called Shingon, but you can find elements of tantra in other — but not all — forms of Buddhism, including Japanese Zen.

Tantra in this sense is not about having exotic sex, sorry. Tantra yoga is also called deity-identification yoga, because the basic practice is to realize and experience oneself as a deity in order to realize enlightenment (*bodhi*, which more literally means "awake"). For example, the practitioner may be assigned a *yidam*, a personal deity that corresponds to the practitioner's personality. Then, through various esoteric practices, the practitioner perceives and experiences himself as the yidam. This process is internal and psychological, not magical, according to everything I've been told about it.

The late Lama Thubten Yeshe explained,

> Tantric meditational deities should not be confused with what different mythologies and religions might mean when they speak of gods and goddesses. Here, the deity we choose to identify with represents the essential qualities of the fully awakened experience latent within us. To use the language of psychology, such a deity is an archetype of our own deepest nature, our most profound level of consciousness. In tantra

we focus our attention on such an archetypal image and identify with it in order to arouse the deepest, most profound aspects of our being and bring them into our present reality.
[*Introduction to Tantra: A Vision of Totality* (1987), p. 42]

Lama Yeshe also suggested that if the iconic Tibetan deities don't
work for you, you might try a western spiritual icon such as Jesus or the
Virgin Mary. He was saying, in other words, that tantra yoga uses "sacred" imagery and archetypes to enable what is essentially a kind of psychological process.

It's true that tantric masters don't always explain it that way. The
formal path takes one through a number of increasingly esoteric levels,
and at the beginner levels the deities often are spoken of as if they have
distinctively "real," separate existence and are out there somewhere.
Foundational Mahayana[xiii] philosophy says that *nothing*, including you,
has distinctively separate existence, however, so this should give you a
clue where this process is going.

The path eventually takes the student to a place where the teachings are intellectually ungraspable, but if she has been properly prepared
she can perceive and realize what the teachings are pointing to.

I've not done formal tantra yoga myself, but I've been through
something sorta kinda like it in Zen. Zen is not at all esoteric, mind you. By
now the entire canon of teachings and commentaries has not only been
published, but much of it has been translated into many languages. The
catch is that most of this canon makes no intellectual sense, and understanding it as it is intended to be understood requires going through a process of deconstructing one's ordinary perceptions of reality.

That doesn't stop some western academics with no experience
with Zen practice from analyzing and interpreting Zen texts intellectually.
The results are, invariably, painfully and horribly wrong, but if you tell
them that they get very defensive and huffy and point to their Ph.D.s, as if
that settled anything.

The third category of Buddhist gods is a kind of grab bag of everything that doesn't go into the first two categories. Throughout Asia, for
example, many laypeople do relate to the iconic characters of Buddhism as
gods in a more standard sense. Students might visit a temple and offer incense to the Buddha for help in passing an examination, for example.

Western convert Buddhists, who can be puritanical snots about
things, sometimes get bent out of shape about such practices because *the*

Buddha isn't supposed to be a god. And *if we wanted a theistic religion, we could have stayed Episcopalians.*

And I say, hey; if it helps give the student some confidence, what's the harm? And who's to say the student isn't relating to the Buddha as an archetype of his own scholarly nature? Further, this is an entirely personal and voluntary practice that you don't have to do if you don't want to.

There's also Amitabha Buddha, a very popular figure in eastern Asia. In some schools of Buddhism it is believed devotion to Amitabha enables one to be reborn in a Pure Land, which is a place in which enlightenment is easily realized. As with everything else, there are a lot of different ways to understand this other than literally. The Pure Land might be a state of consciousness achieved through practice, for example. Of course, lots of people do appear to think of the Pure Land as a physical place.

Like God, the Buddha figure that sits on many altars can be understood in many ways. For example, he might represent the teachings, or enlightenment itself, or all enlightened ancestors, or all beings throughout space and time, or the Buddha-nature that is our original being-ness.

Once I heard someone object to bowing to the Buddha during a Zen ceremony, and a monk answered, "That's you sitting on the altar. You're only bowing to yourself."

Part of the issue with Buddhism is that because so much of it is intellectually ungraspable, and because the perceptual cultivation required to "grasp" it is a lot of work, in many parts of Asia there has long been an attitude that laypeople can't be expected to understand this stuff. So laypeople sometimes were just told to venerate the Buddha, perform certain rituals, keep the Precepts, and give alms to the monks. This leaves a lot of blanks for laypeople to fill in, and they often have done so with folk beliefs and elements borrowed from other religions. It's *sometimes* the case that Buddhism as an Asian socio-cultural phenomenon and Buddhism as a formal spiritual practice tradition based on the teachings of the Buddha bear only superficial resemblance to each other.

I also want to note that Hinduism seems to have developed several dozen different ways to understand "God" or "gods," but someone else will have to explain them. I have just enough knowledge of this that I know there's a lot I don't know.

The last several paragraphs don't qualify as even a beginner-level introduction to god concepts in Asian religions. I'm bringing it up just to illustrate other ways gods can be conceptualized.

* * *

The World of Western Theology is enormously complex as well. I understand that today's basic "standard" concept of God — a transcendent, all-powerful creator-being who willed into existence a world distinctive from himself — emerged from Judaism in the 1st millennium BCE. And as soon as the rabbis presented this concept to the public, people began to come up with *variations*. And they've been at it ever since.

The concept of God continues to change today. However, sometimes it feels as if this process is regressing rather than progressing. If you read the work of even second-tier theologians of the past, and then spend ten minutes watching anything on the Christian Broadcasting Network, you will fear for the future of our species.

Grappling with the nature of the God of monotheism isn't really my thing anymore, but it is other people's thing, and I appreciate their work. I've already mentioned Karen Armstrong's book *The Case for God,* and if this subject interests you I recommend it highly. There's a newer book along similar lines by David Bentley Hart called *The Experience of God* (Yale University Press, 2013) that's also quite good, although I'd recommend Armstrong over Hart to atheists.

Albert Einstein, whom you might recall also dabbled in physics, made some useful observations about God. Einstein was no believer in God, his "God does not play dice with the universe" comment notwithstanding. But he clearly gave God and religion serious thought.

In an article written for the *New York Times Magazine* in 1930, Einstein imagined that primitive religion was mostly about fear and invoking gods for protection. Anthropologists say it wasn't that simple, although I suspect Einstein was at least partly right.

Next came the version of God more familiar to most of us. Einstein said,

> The desire for guidance, love, and support prompts men to form the social or moral conception of God. This is the God of Providence, who protects, disposes, rewards, and punishes; the God who, according to the limits of the believer's outlook, loves and cherishes the life of the tribe or of the human race, or even or life itself; the comforter in sorrow and unsatisfied longing; he who preserves the souls of the dead. This is the social or moral conception of God.

However, Einstein said, that's not necessarily the end of the story.

> But there is a third stage of religious experience which belongs to all of them, even though it is rarely found in a pure form: I shall call it cosmic religious feeling. It is very difficult to elucidate this feeling to anyone who is entirely without it, especially as there is no anthropomorphic conception of God corresponding to it.
>
> The individual feels the futility of human desires and aims and the sublimity and marvelous order which reveal themselves both in nature and in the world of thought. Individual existence impresses him as a sort of prison and he wants to experience the universe as a single significant whole.

That last paragraph strikes me as the words of someone who had a brush with mystical experience at some point in his life.

Anyway, as I said, these are useful observations, and I think you can find examples of all three levels of religiosity represented today in the world's great religions. Certainly there's still plenty of fear-based tribal religion, unfortunately. The enormous majority of religious believers probably fall into the second category somewhere. And even among monotheists you can find people who have moved to the third stage and no longer think of God as an anthropomorphic being, yet remain devout, nonetheless. The last sort of believer isn't even that rare, I don't think.

You might argue, *but you don't have to "believe" there is sublime and marvelous order in the cosmos, because physicists say it's so* (or, at least they did last time I checked), *so why is that religion?* And I say the "religious" element has to do with how we as individuals experience and perceive this marvelous sublimity, and how that experience and perception affect how we understand ourselves and our life. As I said in the first chapter, religion isn't necessarily about believing things.

I've already mentioned Paul Tillich (1886-1965), considered to be one of the great theologians of the 20th century. His seminal book *Dynamics of Faith* effectively skewers both literalism and faith-as-belief, and I wish more people who cite Tillich in discussion forums would read it and stop relying on the outline of his thinking provided by Wikipedia.

For example, faith to Tillich was ultimate concern, in particular an ultimate concern that is "a centered act of the whole personality." He explicitly rejected faith "as an act of knowledge that has a low degree of evidence. . . . If this is meant, one is speaking of *belief* rather than faith."

Amen.

* * *

I've been arguing that it's inane to argue about the nature of God, because there's little agreement even among the religious what God actually is. When people ask, "Do you think God exists?" how can anyone answer without first arriving at an agreed-upon definition of God?

But speaking of the great theologian Paul Tillich and the great physicist Albert Einstein allows me to segue into the next part of the discussion — *What do you mean by "exist"?*

Tillich, in spite of his having been an ordained Lutheran pastor, is intensely disliked in many Christian quarters because he said that God does *not* exist. But Tillich's position was not atheistic. He was referencing the nature of *existence*, which goes right over a lot of heads.

What is it to exist? In March 2013 some physicists, mathematicians and philosophers got together at the Museum of Natural History in New York City for the annual Isaac Asimov Memorial Debate.[xiv] The topic being debated was "The Existence of Nothing," or whether "nothing," in the sense of the opposite of "something," has existence.

And they couldn't agree.

This was partly because they couldn't agree on what "nothing" is. If "nothing" is a void, then a void is still *something*, because it has place and shape, and the laws of physics still apply. But others considered whether maybe there's another degree of nothingness that's even more nothing than a void, although they were having a hard time trying to define that. One theoretical physicist proposed "the ground state of a gapped quantum system," but I don't know what that means. I infer it's when the nothing is *so* nothing that there's nothing left for the laws of physics to apply *to*.

If it's possible that "nothing" can exist, then what is existence? Philosophers have been debating this since the dawn of philosophy, and there's still no general agreement. For example, there is an ancient and ongoing argument over whether existence is a *property* or not, and if it is, is that property intrinsic to or separable from an object that is said to exist (or not)? Saint Thomas Aquinas, for example, thought that a thing's existence is separate from a thing's nature or essence. Many other smart people have disagreed.

The word *existence* is from the Latin *existere*, which means "to stand forth" or "appear." Something that we can conjure only in our imaginations, such as the Flying Spaghetti Monster, does not exist. I think most people would agree with that, with apologies to FSM devotees.

But there are types of incorporeal things that are not imaginary. I understand B.F. Skinner, founder of the behaviorist school of psychology, argued that mental phenomena — thoughts themselves, not just the imaginary objects of thoughts — do not exist because they lack physical qualities. I don't think many hold that view now, but some neuroscientists today question whether there is a clear physical correlation between measurable brain activity and some mental phenomena, such as thoughts. My understanding is that as far as we know, even now, thoughts have no physical or material existence. Would you say that thoughts exist?

I found an article on the *Scientific American* website by Ferris Jabr titled "Why Life Does Not Really Exist."[xv] I'm not going to repeat all of Jabr's argument here, but in short he writes that science still can't explain life or define it according to any physical property, including molecular structure. By most definitions of "existence," life does not exist.

I assume another scientist might argue that we can observe life's *effects*, even if we don't yet know what it is, so it must *be*. And please understand I'm not trying to make a "god of the gaps" argument here, that just because something can't be explained by science there *must* be a divine cause. That's a stupid argument, especially since science is perpetually expanding what it can explain. My only point is that *existence* can be terribly difficult to define, and depending on how one defines it, a particular thing might exist in some sense but not in another one.

And then there's quantum physics, which I don't begin to understand. I have read there is a school of thought in quantum theory that nothing exists until it is observed. I'll leave it to the quantum physicists to interpret that. It sounds like Yogacara philosophy to me, but I'm sure I'm projecting.

Yogacara is a 4th century school of Buddhist philosophy that says that phenomena exist only as objects of awareness (*vijnana*). Awareness in this sense is what connects sense organs (e.g., a nose) to a sensory basis (e.g., an odor) to create a sensory experience (e.g., smell). In modern terms, we might think of vijnana as a neurological process. Thinking also is a sense organ, in this system, and thoughts and ideas are sensory objects.

As I understand it, this philosophical school proposes that all the distinctive phenomena we think of as "real" actually are being fabricated by vijnana. This fabrication *might* be triggered by external stimuli (there is disagreement on this point, I think), but the distinctive characteristics of the phenomena around us that we think are "real" and "out there" are actually being created by "us."

For example, if a tree falls in the forest, and there are no beings with functioning sense organs at hand, then there is no sound, because the sensation of sound is a creation of vijnana. There's also no "tree" if there's no one around to see and recognize "tree." Or "forest," for that matter.

This is not as completely off the wall as it might seem. Modern neuroscience says that much of the appearance of objects is a kind of collaboration between sensory stimuli and our nervous systems. For example, color is something we're fabricating in our heads; it's not intrinsic to the objects around us. Certainly particular stimuli of light and pigment affect our senses, but as I understand it all our senses actually receive from "out there" are stimulating impulses of some sort. And then our neurological system somehow creates a world for us from those impulses. Thus, the "red" in a little red wagon is in our heads, not in the wagon.

Here's another book recommendation —*The Unpersuadables: Adventures with the Enemies of Science* by Will Storr (Overlook Press, 2014). The book is framed as an exploration into the world of people who believe, um, unlikely things — creationism, UFO abductions, etc. But it turns into an introspective analysis of why anyone believes anything, which is much more interesting. Storr does a good job of putting current neuroscience into simple language —

> We think of our eyes as open windows and our ears as empty tubes. We experience the *out-there* as if we are a tiny homunculus gazing from holes in our heads at a world that is flooded with light, music and colour. But this is not true. The things that you are seeing *right now* are not *out there* in front of you, but *inside your head*, being reconstructed in more than thirty sites across your brain. The light is not out there. The objects are not out there. The music is not out here. A violin has no sound without a brain to process it; a rose petal has no colour. It is all a recreation. A vision. A useful guess about what the world might look like, that is built well enough that we are able to negotiate it successfully.

On top of that, the brain is perpetually taking shortcuts. By the time we are adults our brains are well imprinted with patterns and models of what the external world is supposed to be. Much of our brain activity is dedicated to recreating reality to conform to established patterns, not to faithfully rendering what's really "out there." New sensory and other information that doesn't fit the patterns has a very hard time being recognized, because our brains will just re-create the closest matching established pattern. Particularly once we are adults, it's very difficult to experience something that's entirely new.

Further, our brains have evolved to re-create only those "realities" that are important to us and our survival. There are vast oceans of potential stimuli "out there" to which our senses are oblivious.

Speaking of existence — the much more interesting question is not whether God exists, but whether *you* exist. And I'm being perfectly serious here. Current neuroscience suggests that the experience of a permanent self that lives in your head is just another fabrication that gives the other fabrications some cohesion. If "you" are just a sensation being generated moment-to-moment by "your" brain and sensory systems, do "you" exist as an autonomous being? Are you *sure*?

And the moral is, we all believe all kinds of unmitigated nonsense that isn't "real." This is true of atheists as much as "believers." Deal with it.

Before there was Yogacara there was Madhyamika, a 2nd century school of Buddhist philosophy that declares it is incorrect to say whether any particular phenomenon exists or not. That's because no phenomenon has intrinsic existence, or self-essence, but instead is a temporary confluence of causes and conditions.

This is something like the way conditions of wind and tides and water come together to create the phenomenon of waves on an ocean. Since waves have no self-essence as waves, you can't scoop them out of the ocean and take them home and watch them "wave" in your bathtub; once the conditions that create them break up, there are no waves. Well, Madhyamika says all phenomena, including living beings, are like this, a temporary collaboration of conditions without self-essence, and they are identifiable as particular phenomena only as they relate to other phenomena, by their function and position. So, they neither exist nor not-exist.

Those simple explanations do neither philosophy justice. They are both very sophisticated philosophical systems (although still not respected as such in most western universities), and over the centuries some of the most brilliant minds of Asia have analyzed and added to them. Mastering either one is difficult, and I'm not going to claim that I have.

However, Madhyamika and Yogacara were both influential in the development of Zen, and after all these years as a Zen student their perspectives have been incorporated into my "normal." And that makes the "Does God exist?" question utterly nonsensical, to me, even assuming I had any idea what God is.

So the activist atheists, who are so certain God does not exist, and believe their perspective is scientific and rational, need to work on their act. What do you mean by "exist"? Define "exist," please. Then maybe we can talk. Or maybe somebody who cares whether God exists or not can talk.

Over the centuries a great many theologians have proposed that God does not exist because God is not a *being*. A being has fixed diameters and position within a space of time, and God isn't like that. Therefore, God does not exist, but that doesn't mean God *isn't*, necessarily.

This is something like what the Buddha taught about Nirvana. Nirvana is not a place, nor is it confined within any dimension of time. Therefore, it cannot be said to either exist or not-exist.

* * *

Now that you're thoroughly confused, let's go back to Paul Tillich. He said something particularly brilliant I want to quote. Here is Tillich on scriptural literalism, from *Dynamics of Faith* (emphasis added):

> The symbols and myths are understood in their immediate meaning. The material, taken from nature and history, is used in its proper sense. The character of the symbol to point to something beyond itself is disregarded. Creation is taken as a magic act which happened once upon a time. The fall of Adam is localized on a special geographical point and attributed to a human individual. The virgin birth of the Messiah is understood in biological terms, resurrection and ascension as physical events, the second coming of the Christ as a telluric, or comic, catastrophe. **The presupposition of such literalism is that God is a being, acting in time and space, dwelling in a special place, affecting the course of events and being affected by them like any other being in the universe. Literalism deprives God of his ultimacy and, religiously speaking, of his majesty. It draws him down to the level of that which is not ultimate, the finite and conditional.** In the last analysis it is not rational criticism of the myth that is decisive but the inner religious criticism. Faith, if it takes its symbols literally, becomes idolatrous! It calls something ultimate which is less than ultimate.

In short, Tillich says, literalism doesn't make God "real"; it makes God ridiculous.

* * *

If you actually care about a Zen perspective on God, I highly recommend a book written by Zen teacher Brad Warner titled *There Is No God and He Is Always With You* (New World Library, 2013). Warner is a dharma heir of a Japanese Soto Zen teacher, the late Gudo Wafu Nishijima. This makes Warner what is commonly referred to as a "Zen master," a title that American zennies, at least, consider too smarmy for general use. And the title in Japanese, *zenji*, is only given posthumously to the most revered teachers. So I'm not calling him that, and I'm sure he wouldn't mind. "Zen teacher" is the more commonly used title.

In the introduction to the book, Warner explains,

> The thirteenth-century Zen master Dogen Zenji said, "We know that we ourselves are tools that it possesses within this universe in ten directions because the body and the mind both appear in the universe, yet neither is our self." [xvi] The word translated here as *it* is the Chinese word *inmo*, which refers to the ineffable substratum of reality, the ground of all being and nonbeing. To me, this is just another way of saying God.

Many monotheists might agree.

5 Iron Age Morality in a Postmodern World

Failing Dao, man falls back on virtue.
Failing virtue, man falls back on humanity.
Failing humanity, man falls back on morality.
Failing morality, man falls back on religion. — Dao De Jing,
sort of

The snip from the Dao De Jing above (verse 38 in most translations) is not entirely accurate. Most translations say "ceremony" or "etiquette" instead of "religion." But as I understand it "religion" and "ceremony" were the same thing in 5th century BCE China.

I wish religious people would stop saying that one needs religion to be moral. Given that most of the mass violence in the world today is connected to religion; given that sexual and financial scandals involving clergy are as common as toast; and given a complete lack of objective, empirical evidence that religious people are measurably more moral than the non-religious, let's just all admit that morality is not dependent on religion and be done with it. To claim otherwise is an insult to human intelligence.

I say that the most rudimentary thing one really needs to be a moral human being is good socialization; an ability to empathize; a conscience. With those attributes, you'll do right by your fellow human beings a large part of the time, at least. Without them, you're going to be a jerk.

Yes, in various ways morality is important to religion, and I'll get to that. It's also important to philosophy. And it's important to getting along with other people. Forget being punished or rewarded in a next life; if you are a jerk it's going to bite you in *this* life.

And, frankly, if the only reason you behave yourself is that you're afraid God will punish you if you don't, I'd say you've lost the virtue, humanity, and morality ground (never mind the Dao) and are barely a step up from being utterly depraved.

That said, I suspect most of us who are religious can think of situations in which our religions caused us to behave better than we would have otherwise, but clearly religion doesn't guarantee anything. We're all capable of being jerks some of the time, and some of us most of the time, and for that reason having some agreed-upon guidelines for what's acceptable behavior and what isn't can make our interactions with other people more harmonious.

The question is, who gets to make and enforce these guidelines? What is morality, anyway, and why does it have to be religious?

* * *

I'm a writer, so I like to know where words come from. Bear with me, here — the English *morality* comes from the Latin *moralis*, which refers to the proper behavior of a person in society. I understand that to the Romans this was mostly a matter of etiquette.

One dictionary definition of *morality* is "beliefs about what is right behavior and what is wrong behavior." So we're back to beliefs again. What is the basis of those beliefs?

The great and not-so-great philosophers and theologians of human history have written enough about morality to fill oceans, never mind libraries, and I'm not about to review all those perspectives now. But at the most basic level, here are the questions many have asked.

A. Is "morality" something that develops within a society that may be different from one society to another; or,

B. Is "morality" a single, unchanging universal code that applies to everyone, everywhere, throughout time?

Further,

C. Is "morality" mostly a code of conduct generated by a culture that enables people to live in close proximity with a reasonable amount of harmony; or

D. Is "morality" dictated by a Supreme Morality Generator (or God) presiding over all of us?

You've probably guessed that some people would endorse the A and C positions, and others would endorse the B and D positions, although I suppose other combinations are possible. If you're an A/C person, you might decide that "morality" is something every society has to work out for itself, somehow. Indeed, history suggests that morality is a kind of on-going collaborative effort in which humans are perpetually re-examining how we value and treat each other. In recent years there has been a measurable shift in how many people view homosexuality, for example.

If you are a B/D person, however, you might think that God has told us what is moral and what isn't, and that there is nothing for us to do but obey.

The problem with the B/D position is that the B/D folks can't agree on what that single, unchanging universal code actually is. Just as one of thousands of examples, in the years before the American Civil War, several large American Christian denominations actually split in half over the morality of slavery. Remarkably (she said, sarcastically), in communities where parishioners had a vested interest in slavery, the clergy tended to approve of it.

And the fact is, I don't think people who embrace the B/D view actually are getting most of their morality cues from their religions, however much they may think they are. The biblical basis for opposing abortion and birth control is laughably flimsy, for example, and hardly justifies the total war some conservative Christians are waging to deny women reproductive rights.

Where does this certitude come from, then? In the case of religion-based morality, I think Buddhist history gives us one possible answer

Unlike with the spread of Christianity in Europe, as Buddhism spread through Asia there was no single ecclesiastical authority making sure everyone was on the same page, doctrine-wise. In the early centuries, senior monks from many monasteries met at least a couple of times to debate and vote on questions of doctrine, but even that stopped eventually. This means abbots of temples and monasteries often had considerable autonomy to determine what was taught in them.

As temples and monasteries took root across Asia, the many variations of Buddhism soaked up the moral and social attitudes of the cultures in which they were planted. And this sometimes set up a feedback loop in which new monks and nuns accepted the local morality as what the Buddha probably intended, even if that issue wasn't specifically addressed in the sutras or the Vinaya (rules for monastic orders). And, of course, the clerical approval of a moral position reinforced it in the local culture.

So it was that schools of Buddhism separated by distance from each other developed different opinions on homosexuality. Reflecting prevailing local attitudes, homosexual sex among laypeople was considered a violation of the Precepts by clergy in some parts of Asia but accepted as no big deal by clergy in other parts of Asia. This is still more or less the case today, I understand. For the record, there's no indication the historical Buddha or early Buddhist scholars addressed homosexual sex among laypeople at all. And the Vinaya forbids monks and nuns from having sex with *anybody*.

Of canonical scriptures and texts, the only text I know of that forbids homosexuality is a 15th century Tibetan commentary on morality that has long been accepted by Tibetan Buddhists as authoritative. Among other things, this commentary forbids sex between men, but doesn't mention sex between women, I don't think. But it's because of this text that Tibetan Buddhism regards homosexual sex as a violation of the Precepts. His Holiness the Dalai Lama gets called out for this from time to time, but whatever he may think of the 15th century commentary personally, he doesn't have the sole authority to de-authorize it. He has to obtain a consensus among other high lamas, and apparently some of them aren't budging.

What this and other examples tell us is that clergy are susceptible to mistaking their own culturally induced biases as the Voice of God (or Buddha).

* * *

Jonathan Haidt's *The Righteous Mind*, mentioned in the first chapter, presents another perspective on the origins of morality. Haidt provides a strong and rigorously tested argument that we *feel* before we *judge*. The moment we are confronted with a moral question, something in our subconscious or intuitive mind churns up feelings about the question that determine our position. Our rational mind then constructs a narrative that explains to us what we think and why we think it.

This hypothesis certainly explains a lot, such as why the reasons people give for opposing same-sex marriage are so lame. Allowing same-sex marriage somehow damages other-sex marriage? If we let gays marry what's to stop them from pedophilia and bestiality? *Seriously? That's your argument?* Nathanial Frank wrote at *Slate*:

> Indeed, what's most marked about today's homophobia is what a clear expression of narcissism it is, along with how unrigorous its rationalizations are. Homophobic people seem unable to see past themselves, to transcend their most rudimentary emotions and arrive at a place that's often reachable only if we apply a modicum of reason—often spurred by empathy—to challenge old mental habits.[xvii]

However, Haidt says that's basically what we're all doing — allowing our rudimentary emotions to dictate what we think. And the rudimentary emotions come from our cultural programming and many other influences, such as the groups we hang out with. Researchers have found they also can influence people's responses to moral questions by exposing them to foul odors, giving them something pleasant or unpleasant to drink, or even keeping a hand sanitizer within view. Reason actually has little to do with it, however much we might want to think otherwise.

When you understand that much of "morality" is about rudimentary emotions and biases, you might also understand why conservative and dogmatic religions of all persuasion tend to get hung up on sex and on keeping women under control, often going way outside the teachings of revered founders as they do this.

For example — going by the Gospels, Jesus said very little about sex and nothing at all about homosexuality, abortion, or birth control. And we know that there was homosexual sex, abortion, and attempts at birth control going on in his time, and he must have been aware of these things. But it appears he didn't bother to address them.

Instead, he went on and on about loving God and everybody else, including your enemies. He was also big on feeding the hungry, caring for the sick, and visiting prisoners. The episode with the money changers in the Temple suggests he was not keen on people trying to make themselves wealthy on other peoples' piety. For a man of his time and culture he was extraordinarily courteous to women, sometimes speaking to them in public (which was a tad scandalous, I'm told) and telling Martha that Mary didn't have to go to the kitchen to make coffee and sandwiches if she'd rather listen to his sermon.

Flash forward to today's right-wing Christianity. See the difference? Do I really have to point it out to you?

The obsession with sex and repressing women and their tempting ways is one of the most common features of conservative, dogmatic religion, whether we're talking about Christianity or Islam or any other major spiritual tradition. Currently factions within Islam are going to unprecedented and grotesque extremes to subdue women. But I say there are factions within many other faith traditions that differ from the Taliban only in degree, not in kind.

And this tells me that the men in charge of things are channeling their own anxieties about sex and women and projecting them into their scriptures. In doing so, they sometimes wander quite a distance from what their scriptures actually say, revealing how pathologically deep those anxieties are.

It's also the case that most scriptures were written in more barbaric times when human women were considered little different from brood animals, and of course some of these texts do reflect sexist attitudes about women. Clinging literally and dogmatically to ancient scripture as the last word in morality keeps us from evolving socially beyond the Iron Age.

For the record: Although generally it's not so obsessed with sex, much of institutional Buddhism in Asia is still riddled with sexism. For example, the early scriptures tell us that the historical Buddha gave monastic ordinations to women as well as men. [xviii] But in some (not all!) parts of Asia women haven't been allowed to receive full ordinations for centuries. In a few places even novice ordinations are denied to women. In those places, when women do attempt to live as *bhikkhunis* (nuns) without formal ordination, they are not taken seriously as spiritual seekers but expected to clean up after the *bhikkhus* (monks). There are reasons for this obstinacy having to do with ordination rules, but it still seems, um, *unenlightened.*

In other parts of Asia women do receive full ordination and are respected for it. So the denial of ordination to women is not true of all schools of Buddhism everywhere in Asia, but where it is true the patriarchy is very stubborn about keeping women in their place.

* * *

Many branches of science — psychology, neurology, anthropology, sociology, and so on — have studied aspects of morality and have proposed many hypotheses about it. This is interesting stuff. The more I learn about the many ways moral values and behaviors are generated and understood, the more I think religion is not the primary driver of *anyone's* moral views.

As I understand it, current research says humans are not blank slates but are born prewired to develop the social behaviors and attitudes we call "morality." The way the prewired social behaviors and attitudes develop can be affected by experience, however. Whether we grow up to be liberals or conservatives, for example, may depend partly on what kind of wiring we were born with and partly on how we were conditioned by family and society to relate to the world. Religious upbringing might be part of that conditioning, of course.

By the time we are adults, our nervous systems are well trained to churn up rudimentary emotions from our subconscious that are the real determinants of our moral choices. But the same situation does not generate the same emotions in everyone, so we don't always agree on what's moral and what isn't.

There appear to be a great many variables that impact how we actualize morality. Some of us are drawing on empathy more than others, for example. Some of us are more moved by appeals to social justice and equality, while others are more moved by loyalty to established hierarchies and traditions.

Apparently most of us have issues about cleanliness and purity clanking around in our subconscious, but it takes different issues to push our purity buttons. Many have noticed that American urban liberals have a *thing* about food, for example. For them, all the Puritanism that used to be about sex is now about organic/natural/whole grain/gluten free whatever.

Maybe it's because I grew up in the unsophisticated Ozarks and not in New York City, I don't tend to be that picky. Hey, better living through chemistry, I say. I really do know people who seem to be a little obsessive, arranging their lives around obtaining holy food, although there are worse things to obsess over, I suppose. I'm done with hearing people talk about their colon cleanses, though.

Sexual Puritanism is still with us, of course. Some people are very certain homosexuality is immoral, and others think that if two adult people enjoy each other, where's the harm? And you can find both religious and not-religious people on both sides of that divide. The homophobes may be more likely to fall back on religion to rationalize their opinion, however, because there aren't many other ways to rationalize it.

In short, religious people may be rationalizing their moral judgments with doctrine or scripture, but the actual judgments are coming from a more rudimentary place. If current research is correct, it's likely a person with the same wiring and conditioning would make the same judgment with or without religion; he'd just come up with different excuses for it.

* * *

Here in the U.S., the Religious Right's war on abortion is so out of control I say it qualifies as a full-blown social pathology.

As I write this, there is a case before the U.S. Supreme Court arguing the constitutionality of abortion clinic "buffer zones," or laws that keep anti-abortion protesters from physically interfering with people going into abortion clinics. The protesters say they are being singled out for discrimination because clinic employees can be inside the "zones" and they can't.

The reason the "buffer zones" were set up is, of course, that "protesters" were making public nuisances of themselves by physically confronting and harassing patients and staff, blocking entrances to clinics, and occasionally murdering the doctors. Some police departments were spending an inordinate amount of time and resources trying to keep the peace at abortion clinics, and the buffer zones made their jobs easier.

I recently read of an organization called Voice of Choice[xix] begun by a fellow who is the landlord of an abortion clinic. It was bad enough when he got harassing phone calls from "protesters" day and night; but when they showed up at his daughter's elementary school with their dead baby pictures and megaphones to harass *her*, he'd had enough. "Voice" is an organization of volunteers who are provided with the phone numbers of people making harassing calls to anyone connected to a clinic. And the volunteers call them back — politely, I hope, but persistently.

I support the right of anyone to express opinions about anything. If anti-abortion protesters want to protest at the White House, or Congress, or at a state capitol building, or a politician at a public event, go for it. If they want to write letters to the editor and publish books and drop leaflets from airplanes, OK. But when they are harassing and intimidating other citizens engaged in a legal activity, that's not protesting. That's bullying.

And in the case of the more aggressive clinic protesters, their behavior reveals that their true motivations are coming from a dark, hateful and ugly place. There is no morality in that.

Let's try a thought experiment: Let's say a number of people decide that banks are evil. This group then targets banks to picket. But they don't stop with picketing. They chain themselves to doors. They try to stop bank customers from entering. They yell at people to keep their money at home and not let it mingle with the infernal financial system. They set up websites displaying photos and names of bank employees and where they live, hinting that maybe somebody could just eliminate these people. Banks are vandalized and even bombed. Some bank managers are assassinated.

Now, how many *nanoseconds* would pass before law enforcement and the FBI call this movement domestic terrorism and shut it down? No one outside the anti-bank cult would stand for this. But when the context involves women, sex, and religion instead of money and business, some-how, it's *different*.

* * *

In the U.S. many religious conservatives place great value in "moral clarity," which s a state of mind achieved by staking a fixed posi-tion on a presumed moral high ground and then ignoring the details of human life that fog the view.

For example, I have read many essays arguing for criminalizing abortion that go on and on about the humanity of the fetus without men-tioning the pregnant woman *at all*. If she is mentioned, she is considered to be a kind of niggling technicality. Or worse, she is portrayed as either weak-minded or as a selfish and ignorant slut who should be grateful for having someone else make moral decisions for her.

The "moral clarity" crowd must never admit that the woman is a valuable and intelligent human being who may be in a terribly difficult situation, because empathy and compassion for her would block their "clarity."

Of course, maybe she just knows in her gut that it's not the time for her to be pregnant. The moral dogmatist always assumes that what's in his gut overrides what's in everyone else's gut.

For the record, I'm equally uncomfortable with people who sup-port abortion rights and argue that the embryo or fetus is just a blob or a parasite. I've never had an abortion, but I have given birth twice, and my children were distinctive individuals to *me* as soon as I knew they were *there*. I still enjoy remembering how my now 30-something daughter used to kick furiously whenever the obstetrician pressed a stethoscope to my belly. *That's my girl.*

However, most people I know who support abortion rights acknowledge that terminating a pregnancy can be a gut-wrenching deci-sion, and most of them don't consider embryos to be parasites. Their dif-ference with the "moral clarity" club is that they don't consider *women* to be parasites.

In short, moral absolutism requires ignoring genuine human life experience, which can make its rigid application anti-human and oppres-sive. In his book *The Mind of Clover: Essays in Zen Buddhist Ethics* (North Point Press, 1984), the late Robert Aitken Roshi said, "The absolute posi-tion, when isolated, omits human details completely. Doctrines, including

Buddhism, are meant to be used. Beware of them taking life of their own, for then they use us."

* * *

This brings me to my long-standing gripe about the Ten Commandments. If you remove them from the worshipful context of Abrahamism, they aren't that special. I understand they probably were written as much as five centuries after the Law Code of Hammurabi, which contains some of the same prohibitions. So they aren't even entirely original.

I have read lovely commentaries on the 10 Cs written by Jewish and Christian scholars that explain their significance to the development of their understanding of God and morality. I understand the 10 Cs also are discussed in the Quran. So they are very important to Abrahamic religion. I'm not knocking that. What I am knocking is the way some conservative Christians have made them into the be-all and end-all of law and morality for everyone.

For example, claims to the contrary, the Ten Commandments are *not* the foundation of American law. I understand American law evolved mostly from English common law, which appears to have been largely influenced by Norman law, which was introduced to Normandy by Vikings (seriously). There may be some distant influence from Roman law, also, since the Romans were everywhere for a time. The point is that the historical significance of the 10 Cs, outside of their role in Abrahamic religion, is kind of nil, and claiming otherwise is just ignorant.

The Ten Commandments appear to be a product of the late Bronze or early Iron Age, depending on precisely when you date them (historians disagree). How well do they apply to modern times?

Not murdering, not stealing, not coveting, etc. are good ground rules, but again, these are not original to the 10 Cs. But how do they help you when you are called to a hospital at 3 a.m. and told your elderly mother has had a massive stroke and do you want to put her on life support, even if there is no hope of her gaining consciousness? What is the best way to "honor" her in that circumstance?

There's a movement among conservative Christians to post the Ten Commandments in courthouses and public schools around the country, which of course violates the establishment clause of the First Amendment. There have been several documented cases, however, in which people who propose to do this cannot name all ten of the commandments when put on the spot to do so.

Some have actually claimed that the Ten Commandments are not *religious,* even though five of the ten are about honoring the God of monotheism, so it's okay to post them in public buildings. This strikes me as a weasel-word strategy of denying God in order to promote God, which also seems to break at least half of the Commandments right there.

There's also an argument floating around that the Ten Commandments are not religious because they come from God, who rules everyone, and so are not exclusive to any one religion. Your opinion doesn't count if you don't believe in God, I suppose.

What this tells me is that to some people, the Ten Commandments are not a religious text but more of a tribal totem that must be displayed everywhere to secure tribal dominance. The 10 Cs also are thought to have magical power to make people behave just by being displayed in public, which is why they are especially needed in schools and courthouses, apparently.

But in reading the Moses stories in Exodus and Deuteronomy, it seems to me the Ten Commandments were given specifically to Jews. You could argue that they could apply to all God-believers. But the scriptures suggest to me they were not intended to be binding on *everyone,* going by what God said about them to Moses. See Deuteronomy 5, for example. That's just my interpretation, of course.

Several of the basic religious rules are cultural moral rules also, which means the non-religious agree with them. There is nearly universal agreement among socialized humans that lies, theft and homicide are immoral, for example, and of course the last two usually are illegal as well. I also suspect that socialization and peer pressure are more reliable "enforcers" of morality than threats/promises about an afterlife. Some religious people appear to assume that atheists have no moral compass whatsoever, which is nonsense.

For the record, Buddhism has Precepts — there is sectarian disagreement over whether there are five or ten or some other number — that are similar in many ways to the Ten Commandments. Along with encouraging moral behavior, the Precepts are a kind of training discipline that helps one become more receptive to enlightenment. But the Precepts are considered to be a personal commitment, not commandments to be enforced everywhere. I formally received the Precepts (16 in my case) and took public vows to keep them in a Zen ceremony called *Jukai* (which means "receiving the Precepts"). But it would be unthinkable to demand that a non-Buddhist, someone who hasn't taken the vows, observe and keep the Precepts.

There's a lot to be said for thinking of *religion*-based moral rules as personal commitments rather than universal rules that must be enforced everywhere. Particularly as our communities are becoming more and more religiously diverse, and we need to learn to live together without annoying the stuffing out of each other, I recommend it.

* * *

A big problem with defining "morality" according to a rigid list of one-size-fits-all rules from the Iron Age is that there are too many situations of modern life that get left out. End-of-life issues such as when to continue or discontinue life support are examples. That's a moral problem created by modern medicine that prophets of old never had to grapple with.

I also think some situations require more guidance than "thou shalt not." We in the 21st century West often allow our adolescent children to spend all kinds of unsupervised time together with little other direction than "don't do it." Many parents in the U.S. are adamantly opposed to teaching the young folks about birth control and instead try to frighten them with stories of sexually transmitted disease or shame them (girls, anyway) into thinking that if they lose their virginity before marriage they forfeit whatever value they have as human beings and no one will like them anymore.

Copious amounts of data suggest that the keep 'em ignorant and frightened approach doesn't work very well, and that the teenagers are having sex, anyway. Rates of pregnancy and STDs among U.S. teenagers are much higher than they are in teenagers from, say, the Netherlands, where (I'm told) schoolchildren practice putting condoms on bananas in sex ed class.

That said, I respect the concerns of parents who believe that sex is something better put off until adulthood, if not marriage, and who feel that telling their adolescent children about birth control amounts to giving them permission to have sex. But, frankly, unless we all agree to go back to the days of keeping boys and girls separated, we have to accept that many are not going to follow direction. We know this, because that's what's happening out there in Real World Land.

Telling young people scary stories about STDs is not preparing them for the power of sexuality and advising them that sexual desire is one of the most compelling sensations they will ever experience. And this is perfectly natural, and nothing to be ashamed of, but often for many reasons it's in everyone's long-term best interest to not act on it. But if they do act on it, they should understand what they're doing and use precaution. And as a parent I realize this is not an easy thing to talk about to your own children, which is one reason why sex ed in school is a good idea.

Seriously, the only sane alternative to preparing them is to chaperone them 24/7. Take your pick.

Teenagers aren't the only ones who need guidance. For example, back in 2009 Mark Sanford, a governor of South Carolina, disappeared from his job for a week, allegedly to hike the Appalachian Trail. It turned out he was in Argentina with a woman other than his wife.

I actually felt sorry for the guy, because his recklessness suggested he was genuinely in love with the other woman. Hey, it happens. In this case, the governor's political career appeared to be wrecked, although in 2013 he won a special election for a seat in the U.S. House of Representatives. Voters can be forgiving.

I read that the governor was a conservative Christian and even a member of a right-wing Washington clique called The Fellowship that meets regularly for Bible study and prayer meetings. Sanford was loudly called out for hypocrisy, but I wondered if it was religion that failed him, not the other way around. Sometimes things come roaring out of your own id that can knock you completely off guard, and all the commandments in the world might not have prepared you for them.

This is a very common experience of mid-life, actually. There you are cruising through life just as you expected, with the spouse and the house and the career and the 2.3 healthy and photogenic children, and one day out of the blue you fall obsessively in love with an Inappropriate Person. And the more you try to ignore or hide your feelings, the more they overwhelm you. Soon it's breaking your heart to not act on what you feel, but if you do act on what you feel you could lose much of the comfortable life you had built and devastate your beloved children. What do you do?

Obviously, this is a perilous situation, and unless you choose to throw morality under the bus it requires caution and all the self-control you can muster. I also think that episodes like this can be your subconscious telling you that *something* in your life that you've taken for granted needs to be addressed. That something may be your marriage, but not necessarily.

So what is it, then? Only you (maybe with the help of a counselor or therapist) can answer that. And if the something *is* your marriage, saving it isn't necessarily the only moral option. My point is that the list of Iron Age rules can seem clear and easy in the abstract but tend to abandon us when *we're* the ones overwhelmed with a deeply gut-wrenching moral dilemma.

There is plenty of anecdotal evidence suggesting that, as often as not, people who are moral absolutists about others' behavior find ways to rationalize breaking the rules themselves. For example, the Pro-Choice Action Network hosts a web page of stories collected from abortion clinics about anti-abortion activists who seek abortions.[xx] A recurring theme of these stories is that the anti-choice woman has persuaded herself that *her* situation is unique and deserving of special consideration, unlike the other women in the waiting room, who are just sluts.

Of course, anecdotes may be manufactured. Yet there is solid data showing us that rates of divorce and out-of-wedlock pregnancy are higher in conservative "Bible Belt" U.S. states than in more liberal ones,[xxi] and this pattern seems to replicate itself worldwide. For example, rates of abortion in overwhelmingly Catholic Latin America, where abortion is nearly everywhere illegal and harshly punished, are higher than in the United States and *a lot* higher than in mostly liberal and allegedly decadent western Europe.[xxii] More conservative eastern Europe has abortion rates through the roof, however, which drives up the European average.[xxiii]

It appears that when absolutist morality is publicly enforced, actual human behavior — heterosexual behavior included — is driven into the closet, leaving actual humans with no practical guidance in their actual circumstances.

I say the absolutist approach to morality gets everything backward. It creates too wide a gap between public righteousness and what people are really doing in their private lives, so that the moral rules are not really guiding anyone. And when we cede the presumed moral high ground to the absolutists, too often we squelch open and honest public discussion of our real-world circumstances and moral decisions.

* * *

You might remember the fight over Terri Schiavo's feeding tube. If you don't remember — in 2005 a woman, Teresa Schiavo, had been in a persistent vegetative state since 1990. Her husband, Michael Schiavo, spent eight years seeking one treatment after another to help her. But in 1998 he concluded, on medical advice, that there was no hope, and the kindest thing he could do for his wife was to let her go. He petitioned the Sixth Circuit Court of Florida to be allowed to remove her feeding tube.

But Terri Schiavo's parents fought the petition. The court ruled in favor of Michael Schiavo, and the parents appealed. And another Florida court ruled in favor of Michael Schiavo, and the parents appealed. By 2005 the parents had filed 14 appeals. The case was fought in motions and petitions and in front of the Florida Supreme Court. The U.S. Congress passed a highly unconstitutional law that moved the case into federal court, but federal courts sided with Michael Schiavo, also, and the U.S. Supreme Court issued four denials of certiorari in the case, meaning they wanted nothing to do with it.

Meanwhile, an army of "pro life" zealots camped out in front of the medical facility where Schiavo was being cared for, claiming that Terri Schiavo was awake and being tortured by her evil husband who was probably responsible for her condition, and who wanted to kill her to keep money from a settlement that had in fact already been spent on her care. The case completely took over television cable and network political programming for several days.

Television producers booked one right-wing religious figure after another, all taking the side of Terri Schiavo's parents, as if "religion" spoke with one voice on this issue. As I remember it, the "debate" on MSNBC featured a grid of fundamentalist ministers — plus Pat Boone, for some reason — arranged on the screen like a tic-tac-toe board. And the talking heads were all bearing false witness against Michael Schiavo as fast as they could move their lips. It was surreal.

Yes, I'm sure Fox News was even worse, but I didn't have the stomach to watch.

But religion does *not* speak with one voice on this issue. Ministers, rabbis, theologians, etc., *could* have argued on well-founded religious grounds that removing the feeding tube was the moral thing to do, under the circumstances. And, in fact, many members of the clergy said this publicly. But from what I saw the television producers didn't ask not-fundamentalist religious people into the studios.

Remarkably, most polls of public opinion showed that Americans watching this circus sided with Michael Schiavo, in spite of the lopsided media coverage. That gave me hope for the future of America.

However, it would have been *really nice* to have had a fact-based and non-hysterical public discussion of end-of-life issues. It also would be really nice to have a fact-based and non-hysterical public discussion about abortion law and a lot of other issues affecting people's lives. But in the

U.S. it seems we can't have those discussions without the absolutists highjacking them and shouting over everyone else, as they were allowed to do with Terri Schiavo..

According to reports, an autopsy of Terri Schiavo revealed her brain had atrophied and that she had not been sentient for years. [xxiv]

*   *   *

Many lazily assume that if something is immoral it ought to be illegal. I disagree. I see "moral" and "legal" as two overlapping circles making a Venn diagram. There are some things that are immoral *and* illegal, like homicide and theft, but not everything that some religious establishment considers to be immoral ought to be illegal. And there are times breaking the law is *not* immoral (e.g., Rosa Parks, Gandhi, Martin Luther King's arrest in Birmingham, etc.).

I say law requires a tangible civic purpose. There are some basic areas of law that have been with us since the dawn of civilization, because you can't have civilization without them. If murder were not punished, for example, our species would still be living in caves, constantly on guard against the people in the next cave who might kill us and steal our flint arrowheads. Without some basic respect for property rights and contracts there'd be no commerce and little civic infrastructure. And so on.

On the other hand — however much most people might find adultery immoral I doubt there's much support for making it illegal these days. Cheating spouses have always been with us, but they do not disrupt civilization. In fact, enforcing anti-adultery laws might be more disruptive than adultery itself.

There's also no real-world evidence that legal abortion or same-sex marriage cause any tangible or measurable civil disruption or degradation. Of course, whether you think these things are immoral, or not, is a matter of opinion. But where abortion is illegal it just goes underground; it doesn't stop (see Latin America). And homosexual lovers will make commitments to each other and live together, whether legally married or not. Criminalizing these things does not stop them. Criminalization doesn't appear to slow them down much, in fact. And civilization doesn't seem to care. Civilization tends to function more smoothly without criminal undergrounds, however, so it's best to not encourage their formation.

Human life is infinitely complicated and messy, and circumstances have a way of confounding application of one-size-fits-all rules. *Some things people need to work out for themselves.* Sometimes wrestling with a difficult life situation involving moral questions helps us mature, spiritually and emotionally. If we give our moral agency over to the Morality Police we're asking to never grow up.

* * *

"Good" and "evil," or at least how we conceptualize them, are another aspect of morality. And how we conceptualize these things can have huge real-world consequences.

For example, on September 14, 2001, President George W. Bush said this at a prayer service at the National Cathedral:

> Just three days removed from these events, Americans do not yet have the distance of history. But our responsibility to history is already clear: to answer these attacks and rid the world of evil.

Rid the world of evil? That should have sent off nuclear-strength alarm bells, but it certainly got by me at the time. I assume neither the speechwriters nor the speaker put much thought into the implications of these words, and they were just said for effect. But vacuity of thought is not a trait you want in a national leader, especially one who might (and did) hustle the nation into a pointless war. And if President Bush actually believed what he was saying, he must have been suffering from acute megalomania.

Here's another quote: In a *New York Times* column published February 11, 2004, David Brooks wrote, "Some liberals have trouble grasping evil, and always think that if we could take care of the handguns or the weapons of mass destruction, our problems would be ameliorated. But I know the problem lies in the souls of our enemies."

Now, what might we infer about "evil" from these quotations? The first suggests that "evil" is something tangible, with some sort of finite mass and material substance, and if we just work hard enough we can whittle 'er down and be done with it. The second suggests that evil is a quality or attribute that some people possess, and others don't. And once evil has infected "the souls of our enemies" there is nothing to be done but eliminate them.

The problem is that it's likely "our enemies" feel exactly the same way about us. If we were paying attention, history should have taught us that people who create evil hardly ever see themselves or their intentions as evil. Osama bin Laden and his 9/11 terrorists believed their attack was righteous and justified, as did Timothy McVeigh when he blew up the Oklahoma City federal building.

People are seduced into evil because they don't recognize evil *as* evil. They mistake it for justice, or righteousness, or even God's Will. And the seduction begins with the thought that "I'm a good person," and "his hatred of me is evil, but my hatred of him is justified." As soon as we identify ourselves as "good" and the Other, whoever they are, as "evil," we've well on the way to giving ourselves a cosmic permission slip to do *whatever we want* to be rid of them.

I say this seductive impulse is at the root of most of the mass atrocities humankind has inflicted on itself through the ages. That's why the ways we conceptualize good and evil have real-world consequences.

Please understand that I'm not saying people or nations shouldn't defend themselves from those who intend to do them harm. What gets us into trouble is thinking that we're entitled to Holy Retribution or that we are somehow qualified to pass judgments and inflict brutality on entire populations, because *we're the good guys.*

Also, as Hannah Arendt observed of Adolf Eichmann, sometimes "evil" people are those who mirror the values of their peers and culture, without self-reflection or thought of consequence. When we read about teenage boys brutalizing a girl and bragging about it on Twitter, for example, that's what we're seeing. And when other people try to cover up or trivialize the brutality, or blame the victim, that's what we're seeing. Because such acts are an expression of social and cultural values, and approved by peers, they don't *feel* evil to those committing them.

And later, when the brutality has been exposed to the light of day, we want so very much to believe that the perpetrators are somehow abnormal, or monsters, or possessed of some aberrant quality that caused them to be brutal. But most of the time, in truth, there is nothing measurably abnormal about them at all. That's why cultural values — not just the ones we pay lip service to, but the ones we wink at — have real-world consequences, also.

I'm not sure we all agree what evil is. For example, is a natural disaster "evil"? Some philosophers have said so. But if that's true, does that mean the weather or tectonic plates or whatever were infected with evil spirits? If there is no "evil" intelligence directing an event, doesn't that make "evil" nothing but a value judgment we impose on it? That means evil exists only in the eye of the beholder, doesn't it?

It's more useful, I think — yes, this is the Zen student talking now — to appreciate that "evil" really has no substance and no independent existence. Nor is it a particular quality that inhabits people. It "exists" only in intentions, actions and consequences.

If we understand that neither we nor our enemies are intrinsically good or evil, does that change how we see traumatic events? Speaking as an eyewitness, the 9/11 terrorist attack on the World Trade Center easily was the most terrible thing I ever saw, but I honestly don't see why hanging the label "evil," or not, on it makes any difference. It was what it was. But my perspective enrages some people who clearly think it is vitally important to label the thing as "evil," and if we don't we're somehow being soft or letting the terrorists win.

It seems to me there's some sort of magical thinking lurking in there, somewhere.

I used to struggle with passages from sutras about "good" and "evil" until I learned that the Sanskrit/Pali words being translated, *kusala* and *akusala*, actually mean "skillful" and "unskillful." The next time you want to label somebody or something as "evil," try substituting "unskillful." Then examine yourself to see if that changes how you feel about him/her/them/it.

I'm not taking the postmodernist view that good and evil are purely relative. I say that acting selfishly, or with the intent of doing harm, no matter what the rationalization, is *unskillful*, and therefore evil. To me, "evil" is found in the act itself, the harm it causes and in the motivation behind it, but nowhere else. Not even in the "souls" of our enemies.

*   *   *

I still haven't answered the question, *how do we know what is the right thing to do?* What is the basis of morality?

The standard rationalization for applying an arbitrary list of absolutist external rules is that people are wicked and sinful things who are too depraved to be trusted to make moral decisions for themselves.

Shortly before he was named Pope Benedict XVI, Cardinal Joseph Ratzinger said, "Relativism, which is letting oneself be tossed and swept along by every wind of teaching, looks like the only attitude acceptable to today's standards... We are moving toward a dictatorship of relativism which does not recognize anything as definitive and has as its highest value one's own ego and one's own desires."

His Eminence Cardinal Ratzinger was right, in my opinion, to name ego and desire as the two human factors most likely to get us into trouble. However, by now — after we've had a number of centuries of experimenting with enforced moral absolutes — we should have noticed that all the absolute rules in the world don't mean a damn thing when people give themselves permission to not follow them. And ego and desire are famous for handing out permission.

The word for today, boys and girls, is *rationalization*. People can rationalize just about anything if they want something badly enough and can persuade themselves they are entitled to it. Human history shows us that ego and desire inflame the religious and nonreligious alike, to much the same result.

Further, today the authority of religious establishments is deflating like an old tire. So what's the incentive for following absolute rules these days? If we behave will the Good Morality Fairy give us a cookie?

I say that instead of just handing out rules, religion *ought* to focus on giving people some guidance about ego and desire. A little self-awareness about how our own egos and desires jerk us around can go a long way.

Going back to my list of "fallbacks" at the beginning of the chapter — religion also might try helping people cultivate humanity. Compassion is a really good thing to have, too. Most religions have a lot of teachings on compassion. How about dusting those off and having a look, eh?

Notice I'm not even holding out for the Dao. Humanity and compassion will do.

* * *

I'm not arguing to throw out the rules, mind you, because I doubt living human beings ever are completely free of ego and desire. The best most of us can hope for is to learn to recognize and honestly acknowledge when we're being motivated by ego and desire, and then choose to not act on that motivation.

And that's a lot of work, and not everyone is going to be willing to do the work, and not everyone who does do the work will get very far with it. Sometimes I question whether I've gotten very far with it myself.

What usually happens is that the person who adopts a value of compassion, for example, will wrap himself or herself in a "compassionate person" persona. But until he's done the hard and gritty work of examining himself to find the sticking points, all the selfish and ugly things he clings to, "compassionate person" is a fraud who won't survive a genuine challenge.

However, I've seen and experienced enough to appreciate that the only true morality is morality that is an expression of compassion and humanity. Merely following a list of external rules is a cheap approximation of morality. It's what one falls back on when compassion and humanity are lacking.

And *that* said, I say also there is no cheaper trick in the book than declaring one is so enlightened or compassionate that one is no longer obligated to follow the rules. As a *rule* of thumb, if your spiritual teacher ever says such a thing, find another spiritual teacher. And mind your wallet on your way out the door.

If all this sounds terribly ambiguous — yeah, mostly, it is. That's because you and the world and human life generally are very complicated, and where there is complication, there is ambiguity.

I realize people often are uncomfortable with ambiguity. They want clear rules and sharply defined boundaries. They want all phenomena to be properly sorted into their socially acceptable conceptual boxes. That's a *mostly* workable strategy for getting through life, but it's not real. It's an artificial order superimposed on what's really a complex mess. And sometimes failing to accept reality causes more trouble than it solves.

*   *   *

Many have put forth proposals for a secular form of morality, and recently most of these appear to take what's called a "utilitarian" or "consequentialist" approach. Very basically, utilitarianism/consequentialism is results-oriented. There are many variations of utilitarianism, but most of them require applying reason to a situation to do some sort of harm/benefit analysis, and then choosing the course of action that seems to promise the most benefit with the least harm.

In many utilitarian theories there is some kind of sweetener offered for those who make the effort. This is usually a promise of happiness or well-being, either individual or collective, for doing the right thing. And, y'know, if people actually did this the world probably would be a better place. We humans are social critters; we need each other. Living cooperatively and harmoniously with other humans — rather than perpetually trying to rip each other off — maximizes everybody's well being and happiness.

I think utilitarians give people credit for being more rational and less selfish than most actually are, however. And it doesn't account for old-fashioned bigotry. All manner of horrible things have been done in this world by people who believed they were serving a greater good, and not all of those people were motivated by religion.

When I try to imagine a utilitarian morality successfully applied to a population, what I imagine always ends up looking somewhat Confucian, but without the robes and ceremonies. What I imagine would require a very clearly articulated model of what the "greater good" is, with everyone being held accountable for it. It would require everyone to be imprinted with the same cultural values, so that there would be strong peer pressure to comply, and so that people might be willing to make personal sacrifices if the greater good required it. Which sounds a tad dystopian to me, to be honest. If we're going to go that way, let's at least keep the robes and ceremonies, if only for their entertainment value.

The previously mentioned prominent atheist Sam Harris (author, neuroscientist, co-founder of Project Reason) has written about developing a science of morality and a science of human values. He wrote in his book *The Moral Landscape: How Science Can Determine Human Values* (Simon & Schuster, 2010),

> I believe that we will increasingly understand good and evil, right and wrong, in scientific terms, because moral concerns translate into facts about how our thoughts and behaviors affect the well being of conscious creatures like ourselves. If there are facts to be known about the well-being of such creatures—and there are—then there must be right and wrong answers to moral questions. Students of philosophy will notice that this commits me to some form of moral realism (viz. moral claims can really be true or false) and some form of consequentialism (viz. the rightness of an act depends on how it impacts the well-being of conscious creatures). While moral realism and consequentialism have both come under pressure in philosophical circles, they have the virtue of corresponding to many of our intuitions about how the world works.

I don't know about Harris's intuitions, but mine says that to think we will *ever* be able to say that there are *objective* right and wrong answers to all moral questions is right up there with President Bush declaring he will put an end to evil in the world. Ain't gonna happen.

People and life situations are infinitely complicated. I would hazard to say that given the infinity of variables, no two human beings ever faced completely identical moral dilemmas. And I think that we are better off giving ourselves some freedom to be subjective, to consider complex moral questions not just in the abstract but in the light of our particular life and situation. When faced with questions about ending a pregnancy, or a marriage, or when to discontinue life support, or whether to intervene in a friend's problems or let things sort themselves out — we *need* to be able to apply some subjectivity to matters that will change our lives and the lives of those around us, because we're the only ones familiar with most of the variables.

We can, as a society, draw parameters around moral questions — medical guidelines determining when life support is futile, gestational limits for elective abortion, that sort of thing — and then we'll continue to do what we've always done, which is argue among ourselves about where the parameters should be drawn (*what about euthanasia*, for example)? Having to argue with each other is the price we pay for freedom. In many cases science can help us draw the parameters, but within those parameters we need to allow some room for subjectivity.

Such things can never be reduced to a one-size-fits-all formula. If that's where we're going, we might as well let religion keep its copyright on morality. It would save us all the hassle of switching over to another absolutist, authoritarian system that nobody's actually following, anyway.

* * *

Basic Buddhist teaching is that our unskillful (or evil) actions spring from what are called the Three Poisons — greed, anger, and ignorance. Exactly what is meant by "ignorance" is complicated, so to simplify this discussion I'm going to change that to greed, anger and bias. It's not exactly the same thing, but it will get us in the neighborhood of the same ball park. The "bias" includes fear, aversion, and all the ways we protect some idea of ourselves from scary Others.

According to this theory, as long as there is greed, anger, and bias, there will be immoral behavior, religion or no religion, science or no science, rules or no rules. The path to morality, then, must involve dealing with personal greed, anger and bias as well as honoring basic rules and guidelines.

But tackling one's own greed, anger and bias is a lot of work, and this is not work that people can be forced into doing. Those of us who hold this view may be able to lead others along by example, but it's going to be an uphill slog. These days a big chunk of the population seems to have embraced greed, anger and bias as *virtues*. No good can come of this.

Beyond doing the inner work of dealing with our own greed, anger, and bias, Buddhist ethics do have some utilitarian/consequentialist elements. But along with the harm/benefit analysis one must also honestly appraise one's own intentions and motivations, and then weigh all that in light of the Buddha's teaching. Simply following absolute rules, especially without reflection, isn't enough.

* * *

In his book *Beyond Religion: Ethics for a Whole World* (Houghton Mifflin Harcourt, 2011), His Holiness the 14th Dalai Lama proposed that ethics and morality should be secularized. He is not suggesting leaving religion out of morality entirely; instead, he uses the word *secular* to mean mutual respect for all religions and "an inclusive and impartial attitude that includes nonbelievers." It means that religion doesn't get to set absolute rules for everyone.

His basic argument in the book is that we — as individuals, as societies, as a species — should be focused on the cultivation of inner values, compassion in particular, as the basis of morality, and not external rules.

"If people lack moral values and integrity, no system of laws and regulations will be adequate. So long as people give priority to material values, then injustice, corruption, inequity, intolerance, and greed — all the outward manifestations of neglect of inner values — will persist," he wrote.

His Holiness then presents his ideas on how this cultivation of compassion might work, and I'm not going to take the time to repeat it all here. Naturally many of his ideas are adapted from Buddhist practice, particularly mindfulness and meditation, although adaptation of Buddhist doctrines would not be required. Still, I think this is something clergy and other religious leaders ought to be thinking hard about. What is the best way to cultivate the values of compassion and humanity within their religious traditions?

His Holiness Pope Francis has been a model of compassion and humility in his short reign, and the world has fallen at his feet. Catholics and non-Catholics alike express admiration for him. Perhaps it says something about the shallowness and superficiality of our time that people are astonished and inspired by a holy man acting like a holy man, but I feel encouraged. Maybe this will be the beginning of a trend.

* * *

If you *prefer* rules I have another suggestion, which is that we think of morality in terms of what we do rather than what we don't do. By that I mean instead of a list of "thou shalt nots," maybe we should be going by a list of "thou shalts."

The Precepts of Buddhism sometimes are expressed positively as well as negatively. For example, "do not kill" is the negative; "nourish and care for living beings" is the positive.

People may think they've got the "not killing" thing covered by being vegans, but if they're wearing "vegan" shoes made by exploited workers in some third-world sweatshop, not so much.

The negative "do not steal" becomes the positive "practice generosity." Give what you can. Don't waste or hoard resources others might need. The negative "don't misuse intoxicants" (that's Number 5 on Buddhist lists) might become "keep yourself mentally clear and present."

I say a truly "moral" person is not just one who manages to not lie to his spouse or embezzle from his job, but one who works at being a positive force for good.

* * *

My Zen teacher, Ji-on Susan Postal, died of cancer while I was writing this book. Unlike my first teacher, Daido, who had a dramatic teaching style and a knack for saying wonderfully quotable things, Susan's teaching style was more subtle and intimate; more heart-to-heart. So I don't quote her as much in my writing, but that doesn't mean she was any less of a great teacher.

Susan wrote something I want to quote, but I'm hesitating because it contains the dreaded "K" word — *karma*. Nothing reeks of dilettantish New Age flakiness more than karma, huh?

So let me get a short explanation out of the way — *karma* is a Sanskrit word that means "volitional action." A doctrine of karma, then, would be a doctrine that explains the cause and effect of volitional action, especially in a moral sense.

Many religions of Asia have doctrines of karma. However, *it is not the same doctrine in every religion.* The common understanding of karma in the West is, I believe, the Hindu version, or one of the Hindu versions, or perhaps is more Asian folk belief than anyone's version.

The basic Buddhist doctrine of karma has nothing to do with fate. It is not a cosmic criminal justice system. There is no intelligence in the sky directing it. It's more like a natural law of human behavior, or cause and effect. There are other sets of natural laws that cause things to happen as they do, the Buddha taught, so that not everything is the way it is because of karma. Again, the natural law of karma is only about the causes and effects of volitional action.

Everything you do with thought, speech, or action has an effect, and the cumulative effect of all of your volitional actions is what built the life you have right now. Further, you can change the trajectory of your life and your karma by changing your actions. You are *not* fated to suffer X amount of bad things because you did X amount of bad things in the past.

And you don't have to wait for another life to feel the effects of the karma created in this life; the effects begin immediately.

The several schools of Buddhism have myriad teachings on karma, some of which are more mystical, some of which I doubt. Appreciating the Buddhist doctrine of karma on a basic level, however, does not require a psychedelic journey through Woo-Woo Land. Once you understand what it is, you can watch it happen in everyday life.

Karma is enormously important to how Buddhists understand morality. We originate karma and we are conduits of karma, and we can choose to let beneficial karma flow through us to reach others (for example, "paying it forward"), while seeing to it that harmful karma that reaches us *stops* with us and doesn't hurt anyone else (for example, not being angry and snippy half the day because somebody cut you off in traffic).

Anyway, Susan wrote a short *gatha* or verse that we at Empty Hand Zen Center use as our "benediction," the last thing chanted in our chanting services. I think it speaks volumes about basic morality.

The Verse of Gratitude

For all beneficent karma ever manifested through me,
I am grateful.
May this gratitude be expressed through my
body, speech and mind.
With infinite kindness to the past,
Infinite service to the present,
Infinite responsibility to the future.

6 The Crazy Scripture in the Attic

No man in these islands ever believes that the Bible means what it says: he is always convinced that it says what he means. -- George Bernard Shaw, 1895

I've encountered books and websites declaring that Copernicus (1473-1543) ran afoul of the Catholic Church because he said the Earth revolves around the Sun, and the Bible says the Sun revolves around the Earth. But the Bible says no such thing. Whoever wrote the Bible was oblivious to the solar system.

It's true that in a few places the Bible describes Earth as being set on an immovable foundation, and the Sun as rising and setting (as we speak of it today). But by Copernicus's day the Church had accepted that the Earth was round and surrounded by space, not literally set on a foundation, although they were very certain that the Earth did not move. The notion that the Church was still promoting the myth of a flat Earth at that time is itself a myth popularized in the 19th century.

If you look more closely at that episode of history, the Church's real gripe wasn't so much about biblical literalism as it was about ecclesiastical authority. The Church had adopted Ptolemy's geocentric model, which put Earth at the center of the universe, as the correct view. Claudius Ptolemy (ca. 90-168 CE) was a Greco-Roman scholar who lived in Egypt and who had tweaked the old Aristotelian geocentric model in an attempt to account for planetary movements many had observed but could not explain — well, until Copernicus explained them.

Ptolemy? Aristotle? Not Moses or Abraham?

Sometime in the Middle Ages European scholars had rediscovered the classic Greek philosophers and had fallen in love, and they had folded much classic Greek thought into their own thinking, albeit sifted through a proper Catholic filter. By the time Copernicus came along, many ideas originating with pagan Greek philosophers had become official Church dogma. And the Church insisted on being the final, official arbiter of all things, including things we wouldn't today consider "religious." For example, nearly a century later, in 1632, the Jesuit Revisors General rejected the proposition that matter is composed of infinitely small atoms because it was "repugnant to the common doctrine of Aristotle." [xxv]

So the Church's issue with Copernicus's *De revolutionibus orbium coelestium*, which proposed that the Sun is at the center of the then-observable universe, was only partly about the Bible. Mostly, the Church was having a snit because some scientist was publishing texts declaring what was and what wasn't without getting it cleared with the Church first. I have read speculation that if Copernicus had submitted his book to the Vatican for approval before publication, the truth committee may have just said *Yeah, OK, whatever* (*Non erat qui interpretaretur. Approbamus.*), and given it a go-ahead.

Or, maybe not. *De revolutionibus orbium coelestium* was published in 1543, just before Copernicus's death. About 26 years earlier, in 1517, Martin Luther (1483-1546) had issued his Ninety-five Theses challenging Church authority, which touched off the Protestant Reformation. By 1543, hotspots of open revolt against the Vatican were scattered throughout Europe, and King Henry VIII's England already had broken away and turned Protestant. The Church was not in the mood to put up with a challenge to its authority from some nobody Polish astronomer.

The Reformation had not yet concluded when Galileo (1564-1642) came along and supported Copernicus, and the Church was not yet in a forgiving mood. When Galileo published a book that not-too-subtly ridiculed the Church's view of the geocentric universe, Galileo was tried by the Inquisition and put under house arrest for the rest of his life.

Martin Luther is supposed to have said that Copernicus's model of the solar system violated "Holy Writ," based on Luther's reading of the 10th chapter of the Old Testament book of Joshua. Here is the King James Version of the relevant passages:

> And it came to pass, as they fled from before Israel, and were in the going down to Bethhoron, that the LORD cast down great stones from heaven upon them unto Azekah, and they died: they were more which died with hailstones than they whom the children of Israel slew with the sword.

> Then spake Joshua to the LORD in the day when the LORD delivered up the Amorites before the children of Israel, and he said in the sight of Israel, Sun, stand thou still upon Gibeon; and thou, Moon, in the valley of Ajalon.

And the sun stood still, and the moon stayed, until the people had avenged themselves upon their enemies. Is not this written in the book of Jasher? So the sun stood still in the midst of heaven, and hasted not to go down about a whole day.

I don't see how these passages wouldn't have been violated by Ptolemy's geocentric model also, never mind by physics in general, but whatever. This objection to Copernicus is something Luther was overheard saying at a dinner party, I understand. He may have been misquoted.

Luther *is* famous for standing up to the Church and saying that only the Bible, not the Church, is the final authority of truth. Luther called his new church *der evangelische Kirche* — "the evangelical church" — coining *evangelische* from the Latin *evangelium,* derived from the Greek *euangelion,* "the good news." To Luther, *der evangelische Kirche* was a church whose teachings were centered on the Gospels, the "good news." My Sunday School teachers at the Missouri Synod Lutheran Church my family attended assured us that ours was an evangelical church, although standard Christian taxonomy classified us simply as Protestants.

Evangelicalism as a movement distinct from older Protestant denominations emerged in Britain and the United States in the 18th century. Among the characteristic features of Evangelicalism, in the U.S. South at least, is faith in the Bible as the inerrant and eternal voice of God speaking directly to his people. The older Christian denominations certainly place huge emphasis on the divine origins of the Bible, also, but Evangelicals turned that emphasis up several degrees. Arguably, some factions of Evangelicalism eventually turned the Bible into an object of worship in its own right.

*   *   *

In the last chapter I mentioned that before the Civil War some American Christian churches split over the issue of slavery. The splits involved both mainline Protestant denominations (i.e., Presbyterians) and Evangelicals (i.e., Baptists). If these churches were being directed by the same scriptures, how could they have arrived at such an impasse over slavery?

The Bible doesn't exactly give slavery a ringing endorsement, but in several passages it *accepts* slavery, as it also accepts polygamy and the keeping of concubines, which conservative Christians work very hard to not notice. So, southern ministers, many of whom owed their positions to their plantation-owning parishioners, defended slavery. The Bible says it's okay, so it's okay.

A great many historians have proposed that the American Bible Belt was born in the antebellum period, as the religion, culture and politics of the South congealed to form a protective barrier around the institution of slavery. And religious historians have argued that the pro-slavery ministers' reading of the Bible took American religion further down the rabbit hole of literalism. In the southern ministers' view, one need not ponder the deeper meaning of the Word on matters such as loving one's enemies and treating the poor and downtrodden with kindness and charity. Instead, the Bible was to be used to look up facts about God's social and political views. No soul-searching was required.

Matters were much messier in the North. Christian abolitionists argued that their views reflected the spirit of the words of Jesus and the Apostles, even if none of those words specifically applied to slavery. This was a more difficult argument to make, and in many ways they lost that argument even though slavery was abolished. But you have to give them credit for trying to apply something resembling critical thought to scriptures from the Bronze and Iron ages to make them relevant to their Industrial Age world.

In retrospect some Christian abolitionists weren't exactly role models of rectitude, either, to be honest. Evangelicals in particular were as likely to be anti-Irish immigration and anti-Catholic as anti-slavery. For many, the thought of slave plantations filling up the western territories and freezing out (white) family-owned farms and businesses sparked their anti-slavery zeal much more than reading *Uncle Tom's Cabin*.

Even so, the Christian abolitionists were attempting something that still needs to be done if Christianity doesn't want to make itself completely obsolete eventually. And that is to acknowledge that even if we assume God is inerrant, the folks who took dictation to write the Bible had limited knowledge of the physical world and harbored cultural values very alien to ours, and we need to take that into account when we read it.

Many Christians and some not-so-conservative Christian denominations already acknowledge these things and adjust their reading of scripture accordingly. But every time literalists wave their Bibles and make a big bleeping deal about the evils of same-sex marriage, for example, they alienate more and more young people who simply don't share their visceral hatred of homosexuality.

And we keep fighting this fight. First it was slavery, then women's suffrage, then racial segregation, then civil rights for racial minorities and women, and now it's reproductive rights and homosexuality. And every time, literalist Christians fall back on the same basic argument — *some bit of scripture written as much as 3,000 years ago says X, so we say X, too.* Period, end of discussion. But if a literalist reading of scripture says same-sex marriage is bad, why isn't slavery still okay? Or polygamy, for that matter?

Sigmund Freud's "pitiful rearguard action" does come to mind.

* * *

At this point much of Christianity is deeply invested in absolute biblical authority. And exactly how some Christian denominations might maintain that authority while acknowledging there are some things that were okay way back when that are not okay now is, well, not going to be simple. All I can say is — sorry I can't help, Christian dudes. I wish you all the best, though, really.

I do feel compelled to point out that much of Judaism, which shares some of the same scriptures, seems to have found a way to honor the scriptures without being confined by them. As I understand it, the Rabbinic tradition does not allow scripture to harden into dogmas that must be thoughtlessly obeyed, but instead provides a way to keep scripture fresh and alive and relevant to real life.

Although Judaism certainly has fundamentalist factions, most of Judaism seems to get along with modernity just fine. According to a 2009 Harris poll, for example, 80 percent of American Jews have no quarrel with evolution. Perhaps Christians could learn something about how to relate to scripture from this. Just a suggestion.

* * *

I've been carping about literalism, but there are other dynamics at play in reading scripture. And it's time now for a quick review of communication theory.

What is communication theory? Back when dinosaurs roamed the earth and I was a university student, I took a course in communication theory offered by the sociology department. While there must have been a lot in the course I don't remember, what I do remember has been useful to me over the years. Since then communication theory has gone off in all sorts of other tangents that I am ignoring.

Here is the basic Jurassic Model of Communication Theory as I remember it. Communication involves a sender, a medium, and a receiver.

Correct transmission of the communication depends as much on the medium and the receiver as the sender. Communication can fail at any point, for a lot of reasons.

In other words, just because someone did a pretty good job explaining something doesn't mean the audience will understand it. Communication depends on both parties speaking exactly the same language, for example. Communication also can be garbled by the receiver's own cognitive filters and biases.

Interpreting a myth as literal fact is one kind of communication failure. It's also the case that often people see what they expect to see, and not what's actually *there*, when interpreting a message. Mental filters are a big reason why eyewitness accounts of crimes are notoriously unreliable; five people observing the exact same event often will "see" five very different events. General intelligence makes a difference too, of course, but smart people have filters and biases that can be just as stubbornly difficult to penetrate as stupidity.

In the same way, how people understand the Bible depends a lot on how they relate to it, because that relationship sets up all manner of cognitive filters that determine what the reader is able to see and how he or she understands it. This relationship varies widely among the denominations of Christianity. Catholics relate to the Bible somewhat differently from mainline Protestants; mainline Protestants relate to the Bible somewhat differently from Evangelicals; fundamentalists — and no, fundamentalism is not synonymous with Evangelicalism, although there is overlap — relate to the Bible differently from many Evangelicals. These differences in relationship can be subtle, but they do matter.

At one end of the scale, there are Christians who regard the Bible as something like the historical record of God's interaction with humans in ancient times, as interpreted for them by theologians and priests. At the other end of the scale, the Bible is itself an object of worship; a physical representation of God himself through which God speaks. Worshiping of objects thought to possess divine power is one of the older forms of mysticism, yes, although not a form I endorse. Arguably the Bible has been made into an idol by some folks.

When you wander outside Christianity you can find an even broader spectrum of relationship to scripture. Not all religious traditions look to scriptures as God's Word.

I don't know if anyone's ever tried to measure this, but I propose that the more emotionally invested one becomes in a scripture — whether those feelings are positive or negative — the less one is able to read it accurately. And in my experience, the more fanatical the Christian, the less likely that person is to read the Bible in any sort of holistic way. The parts of it that fuel his fanaticism will be memorized; the parts that don't will be a blur. If you open the book for him and point to a passage that clearly contradicts his beliefs, he won't be able to understand its implications and will explain it away, somehow.

Put another way, many Christians have a Bible in their heads that may or may not match the one that gets printed on fine opaque paper and bound into a faux leather case. And the Bible in their heads is the one they're actually going by.

*   *   *

It's also the case that for all our fabled religiosity, Americans on the whole are scripturally illiterate. Polls by organizations such as Gallup and the Barna Group/American Bible Society going back several years consistently show that while a majority of Americans agree that the Bible contains all the answers to life's questions, a larger majority of Americans cannot name all ten Commandments, and only about half can name the first book of the Bible (Genesis).

In his book *Religious Literacy: What Every American Needs to Know — and Doesn't* (HarperCollins, 2007), Stephen Prothero (chair of the religion department of Boston University) wrote that religious faith in America "is almost entirely devoid of content." This echoes the late Susan Sontag when she attempted to explain American religion to a German audience:

> Many commentators have noted that perhaps the biggest difference between the United States and most European countries (old as well as new according to current American distinction) is that in the United States religion still plays a central role in society and public language. But this is religion American style: more the idea of religion than religion itself.
>
> True, when, during George Bush's run for president in 2000, a journalist was inspired to ask the candidate to name his "favourite philosopher," the well-received answer — one that would make a candidate for high office from any centrist party here in any European country a laughing stock — was "Jesus Christ." But, of course, Bush didn't mean, and was not understood to mean, that, if elected, his administration would actually feel bound by any of the precepts or social programs expounded by Jesus....

... This modern, relatively contentless idea of religion, constructed along the lines of consumerist choice, is the basis of American conformism, self-righteousness, and moralism (which Europeans often mistake, condescendingly, for Puritanism). ... The very fact of being religious ensures respectability, promotes order, and gives the guarantee of virtuous intentions to the mission of the United States to lead the world. [Susan Sontag's acceptance speech for the Friedenspreis peace prize, Frankfurt, Germany, October 12, 2003]

I do think we ought to note the difference between American public religiosity, which indeed is mostly bullshit, and personal devotion. I see this as the difference between cultural Christianity and religious Christianity. There *are* communities of the faithful who really do read the Bible and know it pretty durn well. I have met such people. What percentage of people who self-identify as Christians in America also make a sincere effort to understand the Bible and apply it to their lives, however, I do not know.

Cultural Christianity is fusing Christianity, or an idea of Christianity, into one's cultural, ethnic or even national identity without necessarily being all that *religious*. For example, cultural Christians often are people who self-identify as Christians but don't engage personally in Christian religious activities, such as praying (except when prompted), reading the Bible, or attending church with any regularity. This appears to happen whenever a particular religion is very dominant in a culture; many people will automatically identify with the dominant religion without ever giving it much thought.

Cultural Christians can also be fierce defenders of displays of Christian dominance, such as municipal nativity scenes and pre-game prayers before high school football matchups. They may have a vague notion that being able to connect their cultural biases to the Bible gives their biases legitimacy, and if so they use that for all it's worth. They are also likely to be about as sincerely religious as a toaster.

Lots of self-identified Christians combine elements of cultural *and* religious Christianity, of course. Seems to me the more they are of one, though, the less they are of the other. And yes, there are forms of "cultural Buddhism" as well. It appears to be a common phenomenon infesting a lot of populations and involving a lot of religions.

For the record, what I think of as "cultural Christianity" overlaps but is not identical to what's called American civil religion. Exploring the many facets of cultural Christianity and civil religion in America would make a good topic for another book, but it's too much to go into here. The biggest difference, as I see it, is that where cultural Christianity tends to be provocative and tribal, American civil religion works at being inclusive — although it doesn't always succeed — and mostly functions to sanctify patriotism. Singing the national anthem before a sports event or group recitations of the Pledge of Allegiance are examples of civil religion. American civil religion also makes use of the Bible as a kind of symbol; for example, in swearing-in and inauguration ceremonies.

*   *   *

The world's religious scriptures are something like our collective spiritual attic. We've accumulated a lot of stuff up there, some of which is valuable and some of which should have been tossed out years ago.

The scriptures of most religions — including the Bible — are vast collections of texts composed by many hands over many centuries. Authorship was ascribed by legends that don't stand up to modern scholarly scrutiny. Many texts show signs of being rewritten a few times by unknown editors before taking their current form. Decisions about which texts should be canonical and which should not were made centuries ago, often by committees of men nursing long-forgotten political and sectarian agendas and often for reasons that make no sense today.

Further, as scriptures were written in dead or archaic languages by people of long-ago and far-away cultures, modern translations inevitably fail to convey precise meaning. Connotations and idioms are routinely lost or scrambled, and occasionally translators have introduced ideas and concepts not in the original at all that became locked into doctrine. Modern interpretations often bear little resemblance to how a text may have been understood by earlier generations.

Many scriptures contain long stretches of verbiage about people and events of no discernible significance. To return to the attic analogy, these sections are like a box of old, unlabeled photographs of people you don't recognize. They don't mean anything to you, but you hate to throw them out because they must have meant a great deal to *somebody*.

And also among the boxes of old *National Geographics* and chests of moth-eaten linens you find some things that are wonderful and precious that deserve to be treasured and preserved and passed on.

In short, the world's religions have enshrined a vast and very uneven amount of literature as holy and essential and won't let go of it, even when a dispassionate analysis reveals *some* of it shouldn't be allowed outside of a museum bell jar. And I don't see that changing anytime soon.

And because so much scriptural literature is a jumbled, uneven mess that can be interpreted infinite ways, somebody looking for justification to do something horrible can find it in scripture all too easily. And I don't see that changing anytime soon, either.

* * *

Speaking of uneven messes — I see some signs that progressive Christians may be trying to refocus Christianity on the Gospels, placing somewhat less emphasis on the rest of the Bible. The Gospels are, of course, the four books of the New Testament that claim to present the actual teachings of Jesus, in his words. The rest of the New Testament amounts to commentary by other people.

It seems to me to be perfectly reasonable to assume that Jesus' actual words ought to have more importance and authority than what the Apostle Somebody wrote later, even if the Book of Somebody *is* in the Bible. Further, re-focusing on the Gospels has the lovely side effect of allowing for a more critical reading of the parts of the New Testament — and the Old Testament, too, for that matter — that strike modern observers as bigoted and stupid.

For example, former President Jimmy Carter published a book titled *A Call to Action: Women, Religion, Violence, and Power* (Simon & Schuster, 2014). The book argues that Jesus treated women as spiritual equals to men. Some reviewers cried foul, many quoting Ephesians 5:22 — "Wives, submit yourselves to your own husbands as you do to the Lord." But those were Saint Paul's words, not Jesus'. There *is* a good argument to be made that Jesus treated women as spiritual equals to men, especially considering the gender role constrictions of his culture.

* * *

One thing Jesus and the Buddha had in common is that neither one spoke English. Most scholars believe Jesus probably spoke a language called Aramaic, but that the Gospels originally were written in Greek, probably by Greek-speaking gentiles who had not witnessed Jesus themselves but were going by what they'd heard from others. I understand another pool of scholars thinks the earliest Greek texts actually were translations of a lost Semitic original, but I don't know how widespread that notion is. I suspect this is wishful thinking.

It's fairly certain the Gospel writers got their Old Testament references out of a Greek translation called the Septuagint that wasn't famous for its accuracy. The original Hebrew verse from Isaiah that prophesied the Messiah would be born of a virgin actually says "young woman," not "virgin," for example. Then all that has been re-translated into Latin and other languages umpteen times, and things *always* get lost in translation.

Nearly every time a new translation of the Bible is published *somebody* gets pissed off about it and assumes some pointy-headed publisher is trying to change the original. The truth is, there may not be an original, exactly. My understanding is that there is no single ancient text that corresponds to the Bible as Christians know it today. The current Bible was pieced together from multiple sources.

Not all translations are translating the same source material, in fact. The venerated King James Version (KJV), published in 1611, was translated from the oldest authoritative source texts available at the time, I've been told, but since then scholars and archeologists have discovered even older documents, particularly of the books of the New Testament, that presumably are closer to the hypothetical original. So newer translations are not just updating the Elizabethan language; they are translating from different sources.

So if your religious faith depends on knowing *exactly* what was written in the Bible — um, maybe you should rethink that.

The Buddha possibly spoke a language similar to Sanskrit, although no one knows for certain. For about four centuries after he died (ca. 5th or 6th century BCE) his collected sermons and the rules he made for the monastic orders — in Pali, the Sutta-pitaka and Vinaya-pitaka, respectively — were remembered through oral tradition. This means they were memorized and chanted, but not written down. A third collection of texts, the Abhidhamma-pitaka, was added to the oral tradition in the 3rd century BCE. The three collections together are called the Tipitika.

After awhile, as Buddhism spread widely across Asia, these chanting traditions were being maintained in at least two languages and probably more. One of these languages was Pali, which is a cousin to Sanskrit, and in the 1st century BCE, in what is now Sri Lanka, the Pali Canon finally was committed to writing. However, the oldest extant copy of the Pali Canon is only a few centuries old, and we do not know how closely that copy resembles the 1st century BCE version.

There were probably several separate Sanskrit chanting traditions, but what we have of those has been pieced together mostly from Chinese translations made in the early 1st millennium CE. Only fragments of what might be original Sanskrit remain. Corresponding Pali and Sanskrit/Chinese versions of the same text usually bear a resemblance to each other, sometimes even a close one, but are not identical. Which version is more true to the "original" mostly is a matter of opinion, although I understand there's a broad consensus among historians that the Sanskrit/Chinese Vinaya is older than the Pali Vinaya.

Today the Pali Canon is the sole scripture of Theravada Buddhism, which is the dominant school of Buddhism in Burma (Myanmar), Sri Lanka, Laos, Thailand and Cambodia. Sections of the Pali Canon were the first Buddhist scriptures to be translated into English, ca. 1880.

A look at these early translations reveals why idioms can be tricky. One Pali word that comes up frequently, *upekkha*, was first translated as "detachment." Later translations, however, usually render upekkha as "equanimity." Not even close. How did that happen?

It turns out upekkha connotes viewing something from a great height, such as standing on a mountain top and looking down at a valley. To the Europeans who first translated the Pali Canon, this suggested "rising above" the events of the world. Hence, detachment. But to Asians, it suggested a broad perspective, or seeing the "big picture," and maintaining a balance between extremes in views. Hence, equanimity.

We see something similar in the Pali Maha-parinibbana Sutta, which tells the story of the Buddha's final days and death. As the Buddha was giving his monks his final teaching, he advised them to "be islands unto yourselves." To a western English speaker this is a bit harsh; "island" connotes isolation, being cut off from others. But to the Pali speakers of southeast Asia, an island was a place of refuge and safety, which also better fits the surrounding context of the advice. At least one English translation I've seen changes "island" to "light" — "be lights unto yourselves" — which arguably is closer (to an English speaker) to what the Buddha meant.

Another example of a translation glitch is use of the English word *mind* to stand in for three different Pali words that don't mean precisely the same thing. These three words — *citta, vinnana,* and *mano* — have multiple meanings themselves, but none line up exactly with *mind* as English language dictionaries define the word. And this is huge, because the Buddha talked a lot about "mind." But some English translations don't provide a clue which "mind" is being translated, so the reader has to guess if the

Buddha was talking about cognition, or subjective experience, or consciousness, or sometimes what modern readers would think of as neurological processes and not "mind" at all.

I know that translations of the Bible and other scriptures share similar glitches. For example, the Greek *agape* in 1 Corinthians 13:4 sometimes turns up as "love" and sometimes "charity," but I understand most 1st century speakers of common Greek might have understood it as something like "good will." I find it useful to compare two and even three translations of the same passage sometimes, and I recommend doing that with the Bible also, but that's probably going to frustrate those who have believed all their lives that *their* Bible is the absolute and infallible Word of God without ambiguities. They'll demand to know which version is "right," and perhaps none of them are, entirely.

In case you are wondering, beside Theravada there is another major school of Buddhism, Mahayana, that is dominant in China, Tibet, Korea, Japan, and some other places. Mahayana takes in Zen and Tibetan Buddhism and several other sub-schools and sub-sub-schools. Parts of the Sanskrit/Chinese canon, especially the Sanskrit/Chinese Vinaya and some of the historical Buddha's sermons, are important to many schools of Mahayana. And much of the Pali Canon is also greatly respected in Mahayana. But for the most part Mahayana relies on entirely different scriptures believed to have been composed between the 1st century BCE and the 5th century CE. I plan to discuss these a bit later.

* * *

While I'm on the subject of the Pali Canon — westerners who flirt with Buddhism often fall in love with a passage from the Kalama Sutta, one of the Buddha's sermons recorded in the Pali Canon. If you want to look it up, it's in the Sutta-pitaka, in a section called the Anguttara Nikaya, third book, 65th *sutta* (sutra or sermon), usually cited AN 3:65, although there are other citation systems one runs into sometimes. It's complicated.

Or, you can just google "Kalama Sutta"; there are several translations online.

Anyway, in this passage the Buddha *appears* to be saying that people can just ignore scriptures if they want to. Here's a representative rendering of this passage, as it is often pasted into Web discussion forums —

> Don't blindly believe what I say. Don't believe me because
> others convince you of my words. Don't believe anything you

see, read, or hear from others, whether of authority, religious
teachers or texts.

You can see why westerners love this passage. We like to tell ourselves we are free thinkers who make up our own minds about things,
even though that's, um, hardly ever true. However, the translation above
is wildly inaccurate even by scriptural translation standards.

In this sermon, the Buddha is addressing a group of people called
the Kalamas, who complain that every holy man who wanders through
their territory is selling a different set of doctrines. They ask the Buddha
what to believe. And he begins with the mis-rendered passage, saying,

> So in this case, Kalamas, don't go by reports, by legends, by
> traditions, by scripture, by logical conjecture, by inference, by
> analogies, by agreement through pondering views, by proba-
> bility, or by the thought, "This contemplative is our teacher."
> [Thanissaro Bhikkhu translation [xxvi]]

In other words, do not put blind faith in teachers or texts; but also
do not put blind faith in logic, or the odds, or "figuring it out." The translator comments,

> When the Buddha says that you can't go by logical deduction,
> inference, or analogies, he's saying that you can't always trust
> your sense of reason. When he says that you can't go by
> agreement through pondering views (i.e., what seems to fit
> in with what you already believe) or by probability, he's say-
> ing that you can't always trust your common sense. And of
> course, you can't always trust teachers, scriptures, or tradi-
> tions. So where can you place your trust?" [Thanissaro
> Bhikkhu, "Lost in Quotation," Access to Insight [xxvii]]

"Where can you place your trust?" — Now, there's a great question.
The Bhikkhu's short answer was "You have to put things to the test in
your own thoughts, words, and deeds, to see what actually leads to suffering and what leads to its end." If you read the whole sutta — and it's brief,
so that won't take long — you see that the Buddha provides rigorous criteria for determining what is right or wrong, or rather, skillful and unskillful. He wasn't just saying, "Whatever pops your cork."

* * *

Everybody knows that as soon as Charles Darwin published *On the Origin of Species* (the original title) in 1859, Christians slammed Darwin's work because it violated a literal reading of the book of Genesis. And they've been at war over it ever since.

However, that's not precisely what happened.

It's true that since the 16th century Christians had gradually taken to reading the Bible in a more literal, rather than mythological, way. But in 1859, the belief that the *entire* Bible had to be the literal and precise truth, without allegorical or mythological meaning, was still a fringe view. It wasn't until a few years after *Origin of Species* was published that biblical literalism caught on in a big way in the U.S. and then spread elsewhere. The fundamentalist movement was a major promoter of absolute literalism, but fundamentalism didn't become a force to be reckoned with until the beginning of the 20th century.

From its beginnings in the 1870s and 1880s, Christian fundamentalism in the U.S. was a reaction to several social, cultural, and other changes in American life. The huge influx of mostly Catholic and Jewish immigrants in the late 19th and early 20th centuries caused great unease among conservative white Protestants and Evangelicals, for example. Then progressive Christians launched the "social gospel" movement that focused on matters such as improving living conditions in slums and ending child labor, which inflamed conservative sensibilities even more. And there were more direct challenges to religion itself, such as "higher criticism," an academic movement that dismantled old assumptions about the authorship of books of the Bible. Mixed into this were long-standing resentments of urban elites that were common among less sophisticated rural Americans. And it's probably no coincidence that fundamentalism caught on most strongly in the former Confederate states, where many people were nursing many grievances about how the world was changing, and where antebellum support for slavery among Christians had already tilted Bible reading in a more literalist way.

I'd also like to point out, once again, that while the Christian creation myth was adapted from Judaism, Judaism itself has handled the science versus scripture issue more gracefully, on the whole, it seems to me. There are differences of opinion and interpretation, but *most* of Judaism seems to have adjusted to science, in one way or another, with much less struggle than is true for conservative Christianity. This suggests to me that scriptures alone are not the problem.

In the U.S., the post-Civil War years saw the beginning of a kind of feedback loop, in which alarm about challenges to conservative social "norms" and the reaction of conservative Christianity to science began to reinforce each other, creating an increasingly extremist movement. And whether the initial spark that created the loop was more about religion or more about social and cultural bias is debatable. I think it even could be argued that the original Christian fundamentalist movement was pulled together in the late 19th century to sanctify racism and nativism and to stop the march of modernity generally.

Indeed, the time lag between the publication of *Origin of Species* and the Christian literalist blowback reminds me of Jonathan Haidt's proposal that most of our moral decisions are being made with our emotions, and our reasons for our moral decisions are made in support of our emotions. If you look closely at the period, it's true that many people had a negative, visceral reaction to the idea of human evolution immediately following the publication of *Origin of Species*. However, it took awhile before large numbers of people rallied around a popular collective *reason* for that reaction.

The fight over evolution eventually became the most volatile component of the rise of fundamentalism. However, Richard Hofstadter's classic *Anti-Intellectualism in American Life* (Vintage Books, 1962) makes it clear the evolution fight from the beginning was not *just* about religion. More than anything else, this was a fight over modernity itself. Hofstadter wrote,

> One can now discern among them the emergence of a religious style shaped by a desire to strike back against everything modern — the higher criticism, evolutionism, the social gospel, rational criticism of any kind. In this union of social and theological reaction, the foundation was laid for the one hundred per cent mentality.

As time went on the fundamentalists became more shrill. Hofstadter continued,

> The feeling that rationalism and modernism could no longer be answered in debate led to frantic efforts to overwhelm them by sheer violence of rhetoric and finally by efforts at suppression and intimidation, which reached a climax in the anti-evolution crusade of the 1920's.

Hofstadter provides a detailed account of the famous Scopes Trial of 1925 to argue that while the trial appeared on the surface to be about religion versus science, it was really about a backlash to "intellectualism," the sense that those overeducated snots in cities were forcing good, plain-thinking heartland Americans in a direction they did not want to go.

About that same time the Ku Klux Klan was riding a wave of popularity fueled by the anti-modernity movement. The Klan expanded from terrorizing African-Americans in the South to being a genuine national movement that championed Christian fundamentalism, patriotism, and Prohibition. They also disparaged immigrants, urban "elites" and intellectuals. And, of course, their signature issue was still racism. It is believed that by the mid-1920s, approximately 4 to 5 million American men nationwide were involved with the Klan.

Religion may have supported the Klan, but religion also fought back. Some prominent Protestant ministers and the Jewish Anti-Defamation League, along with the National Association for the Advancement of Colored People, spoke out against the Klan, and this seems to have slowed its growth. Then in 1925 the Grand Dragon of Indiana was convicted of raping and causing the death of a white schoolteacher. And a couple of years after that a wave of Klan violence in Alabama was horrible enough to cause revulsion nationwide. The Klan shrank back to its base in the South, where it continued its brutality toward African Americans while also stunting the economic prospects of southern working-class whites by fighting the spread of labor unions.

* * *

I understand there's a common folk belief among atheists that Christians don't actually read the Bible, because if they read it they would see how full of contradictions it is and become atheists.

Anyone who believes that doesn't know human nature from hummus. When people are deeply and personally invested in believing that X = Y, they are unlikely to notice that X is *not* Y, no matter how big the difference between X and Y.

By deeply and personally invested, I mean that if your self-identity and most of the way you sort reality in your head *depends* on X being Y, then your brain will arrange for you to see that X is Y, even if it plainly isn't to other people. And I'm not talking about psychosis. *We all do this*, to one extent or another, about all manner of things.

Trust me, you don't have to be religious to be deluded. People lie to themselves all the time about their money and their marriages and politics and their appearance and whether their teenage children are doing drugs even when the evidence is all over the house. Et cetera, et cetera.

As I think I already said in another chapter, we all live in a fog of projections, and those projections are made up of who we think we are and how we think the world is supposed to be. Some of our projections may be "real" in a kind of relative sense, or not, but none of them are absolutely real.

Indeed, I've come to appreciate that no two human beings live in exactly the same world, although most of the time our reference points are similar enough we don't smack into each other too much. And when we do smack into each other, it's the other guy's fault, right?

As I've been saying throughout this book, the notion that the Bible must be absolutely and literally factual actually doesn't go back all that far in Christian history. And today there really are Christians who fully acknowledge the scriptural glitches, and make allowances for them, even though many don't. But I've tried to make these points to activist atheists in the past, and they *will not* see them. They're too heavily invested in the belief that all religious people are stupid and/or crazy and always have been, and that they themselves are utterly objective, noble warriors of rationalism, or something.

And it's all play-pretend; it's just that the activist atheists and the dogmatic religionists are starring in different plays.

If you have spent your life among literalist Christians you have been well conditioned to accept whatever you read in the Bible as true, and your cognitive filters will resolve the contradictions for you, or not let you see them in the first place. Likewise, if you are a religion-hating atheist reading the Bible, the contradictions and fallacies will stand out like a clown car in a funeral procession. But very likely that's all you'll see.

I actually don't spin my wheels over the Bible much anymore, and I'm sure I've forgotten a lot of it. But when I was growing up in the Bible Belt I knew the Bible pretty well, or thought I did. But once when was still in my teens I realized a verse I was certain said X actually said Y — the details don't matter now — and I was a bit shaken by this. I realized that I had been reading something into the verse that just plain wasn't there.

So to get to the bottom of things, I determined to clear my head of what I expected the text to say, pretend I'd just dropped in from Mars and had never heard of this Jesus guy, and read the Gospels (a Revised Standard Version) from beginning to end with as completely an open a mind as I could muster. And when I was finished, I was absolutely certain that *nobody* had gotten Jesus right.

The most disturbing thing I realized was that Jesus appeared to believe the apocalypse or something like it was going to happen soon, within the lifetimes of the people he spoke to, which meant that he was fallible. Further, his many talks about the Kingdom of Heaven didn't seem to be just about the afterlife heaven, but something else, although it wasn't clear to me what that was. And he was keen on people loving God and getting along with each other, but the redemption of sins thing seemed tacked on, almost an afterthought, and not his central message..

That was the beginning of me going off in another direction. And whether I'd see the same things if I read the Gospels now, I have no idea. *But I'd read all of the same passages before.* I just hadn't *seen* them before.

My larger point is that if a person has been conditioned to understand the Bible a certain way, that's almost certainly going to be how he interprets it when he reads it, no matter what the words actually say. Because *that's what people do.*

Or, put another way, all but the most disinterested Bible reader will see what he expects and wants to see in it. To some it isn't just a book, remember. *This is God talking.* To someone deeply immersed in conservative Christian culture, his whole world, including his own self-identity, depends on the Bible being God's living truth. And because of this, he can't see it as-it-is. It becomes a projection screen that shows him what he expects to see and what he wants to see.

*   *   *

If you think Christian scriptures are messy and crazy, let me tell you about mine.

The riotously diverse schools of Mahayana Buddhism have their own riotously diverse canons of scriptures. As I mentioned earlier, Mahayana Buddhism has developed a large body of sutras thought to have been written sometime between the 1st century BCE — about four centuries after the life of the Buddha — and the 5th century CE. A few may date to as late as the 7th century CE, I understand.

Among these are some of the sutras best known in the West, such as the Lotus, the Heart, the Diamond, the Flower Garland, the Vimalakirti and the Lankavatara. These sutras are not respected as authentic in Theravada Buddhism, however.

Mahayana Buddhists have crafted all kinds of myths explaining how these sutras might be connected to the historical Buddha. Some were said to be guarded in underwater palaces by snake-beings called *nagas* until humankind was ready to receive their teachings, for example. In modern terms, let's just say the authorship and provenance of most of these sutras are unknown. But there's a lot of *really good stuff* in many of the Mahayana sutras, so we keep them and pass them on to the next generation.

Here is an important point: The scriptures of many religions take their authority from being the presumed word of God or a particular revered prophet. Although some schools of Mahayana maintain the fiction that their sutras are records of the historical Buddha, these days most acknowledge that we don't know the identities of the authors, although the teachings in them may be attributed to Buddha in a mystical sense. More than anything else, the authority of Mahayana sutras comes from the wisdom in the texts themselves, as confirmed by many generations of dharma teachers who wrote commentaries about them and required students to study them.

But not every old text with the word *sutra* in the title has achieved equal confirmation.

As each school of Mahayana has its own scriptural canon, a sutra important to one school of Mahayana may be unknown in another. Most of Japanese Buddhism venerates the Lotus Sutra, for example, while Tibetan Buddhism appears to ignore it. Some of the better known Mahayana sutras are respected and studied by more than one school, so the canons do overlap. It's also the case that teachers within the same school may hold different views on which sutras are deserving of study, so the canons are not necessarily rigidly fixed.

But no one Mahayana sutra is equally authoritative in every Mahayana school, and one can find some obscure old sutras that appear to have no official connection to any existing Mahayana school.

And I have to say the quality of these texts varies widely. Some are brilliant, but some strike me as just odd. The best of them engage the reader on a level that is more intuitive than conceptual, however, so they defy standard literary explication.

I do not have exhaustive knowledge of all of the Mahayana sutras, although I doubt anyone does. It's hard to pin down exactly how many Mahayana sutras there are. (The only source I could find hazarding a guess was Wikipedia, which says "about 100.") There may have been more, as over the centuries some major libraries and manuscript collections were destroyed in wars and invasions, and no doubt there were many texts that didn't survive to our time.

In fact, nearly always the earliest extant version of any particular Mahayana sutra is a Chinese translation of a now lost Sanskrit original. If there is a Sanskrit version floating around somewhere, nearly always the Sanskrit text we have today is not the original but a translation of the Chinese translation. This is so pervasive that there is a growing suspicion among historians that sometimes the Chinese "translation" may in fact *be* the original, and the author claimed it to be a translation from an Indian Sanskrit text to give it more authority. And if *that's* true, then sutra writing may have been something of a cottage industry in first millennium China.

On the other hand, the Tibetans say their translations of sutras are also of the lost Sanskrit originals, and if that's so, comparison of Tibetan and Chinese versions ought to tell us a lot about the lost Sanskrit originals.

I occasionally stumble across a Mahayana sutra that may have been influential at one time but is mostly ignored today — well, except for historians and religious studies Ph.D. candidates looking for a unique dissertation topic. There's an annoying tendency among some western scholars to treat every sutra as equally authoritative, when they may be referencing a text that's been gathering dust in the attic, so to speak, for centuries. I've waded through a couple of academic papers on some obscure Mahayana text in which the author does not bother to clarify whether the sutra being discussed is or ever was canonical to any Mahayana school, particularly to a school that still exists or was a forerunner of a school that still exists, which I think is rather important information if you're going to draw broad conclusions about Buddhism from it.

It's not at all unusual for a doctrine presented in one Mahayana sutra to be refuted by another. For example, a few Mahayana sutras suggest that women must be reborn as men to enter Nirvana. But a passage in Chapter 7 of the Vimalakirti Sutra, a highly regarded sutra included in a lot of canons, clearly and explicitly says otherwise. And since Nirvana isn't a physical place, it hardly makes sense to think that it can be "entered" with a physical, gendered body, anyway.

For this reason, sometimes one must make judgments about which teachings are expressions of wisdom and which are not. In Buddhism, it's okay to do that. The Buddha encouraged it, actually (see earlier reference to the Kalama Sutta).

Several of the Mahayana sutras are filled with lavish allegorical imagery, often pointing to teachings that are intellectually ungraspable. For this reason, an unlearned person whose head isn't screwed on all that well could read just about anything into them.

I once ran into a fellow who told me he had read the Diamond Sutra — a short but *steep* text — and recognized that it was a prophecy of the coming of Jesus. If you are even slightly familiar with the Diamond Sutra you will suspect, as I did, that this fellow was psychotic. His interpretation goes *way* beyond merely seeing the face of Jesus on a toasted cheese sandwich. It's more the equivalent of seeing a toasted cheese sandwich tap dance and whistle "Yankee Doodle." And when I pointed out that the Diamond probably wasn't written until the 2nd century CE, if then, he accepted this as even *stronger* proof that the Diamond was a prophecy of the coming of Jesus, since by then everyone knew Jesus had already arrived.

As with all scriptures, English translations are unreliable. I've been told that it's just about impossible to translate early 1st millennium Chinese into standard English, because the syntax of early written Chinese is so alien to that of English that translators must add many phrases and clauses that aren't in the Chinese at all in order to craft coherent English sentences.

In crafting these coherent English sentences, then, the translators often have to guess at what the author meant, and these guesses are based more on the translators' understanding of the teaching than on the words themselves. And translators are sometimes clueless. Particularly when the original is describing something intellectually ungraspable, sometimes the translators' helpful attempts to write something that "makes sense" completely obliterates the subtle, intuitive teaching that generations of Asian Buddhists have found in that text.

However, as I've said, Buddhism doesn't have the same relationship with its scriptures that many other religions have with theirs. Buddhist sutras aren't the Word of God. On the whole, sutras are guides to discerning truth for oneself, not stories and doctrines to be accepted blindly on authority.

* * *

Darren Aronofsky's film *Noah* was released in March 2014 and was immediately banned in several Muslim countries and denounced by some right-wing Christians for being anti-God. Paramount Studios managed to keep the U.S. backlash to a minimum with some smart pre-release outreach to conservative Christian groups, but you can never please everybody.

Some of the expressions of outrage struck me as being unintentionally hilarious. This one is from the Breitbart.com site, in "'Noah' Review: Brilliantly Sinister Anti-Christian Filmmaking" by John Nolte: "Aronofsky's blasphemous claim that God is some kind of tree-hugger who wiped out humanity in the Flood to save the planet and punish Man for hunting animals is a bald-faced lie," Nolte says, and we know this because there's nothing about spotted owls in the Ten Commandments. [xxviii]

And at the World Net Daily website, Larry Stone writes in "'Noah' Revives Ancient Enemy of Christianity" that the film is based on Kabbalah and/or Jewish Gnosticism. Stone writes that the film's frequent reference to "the Creator" is a giveaway. But isn't the Creator another name for God? Not at all; in Gnosticism, Stone says, the Creator is the ignorant, bastard son of a low-level deity, and obviously that's the Creator spoken of in the *Noah* film. [xxix]

I do miss the old *Weekly World News* tabloid with the Bat Boy stories. There was a level of demented genius to *WWN* that Nolte and Stone don't quite reach.

Dan Mathewson, an associate professor of religion at Wofford College, wrote quite a good analysis of the objections to *Noah* for the website Religion Dispatches. In *"Noah, Cosmos* Controversies Not About Biblical Literalism,"[xxx] Mathewson points out that there have been other biblical films that took all kinds of liberties with the original story to which conservative Christians did not object.

Indeed, if you look back at the films from the 1950s golden age of biblical epics, faithfulness to the source text often was the least of their, um, virtues. But nobody seemed to mind. On the other hand, Martin Scorsese's *The Last Temptation of Christ* (1988), which wasn't pretending to be biblically literal, was denounced as evil on wheels, although its actual message was thoroughly, conventionally orthodox, it seemed to me. The suggestion that Jesus might have *considered* having sex even if, presumably, he didn't, made heads explode.

Mathewson argues that Mel Gibson's *The Passion of the Christ* (2004) also invented some plot and injected "a heavy-handed dose of the director's editorial pizzazz" along with "a spiritual message foreign to the biblical text." But this raised no objections from the Christian Right. I remember about the time *Passion* was released spending a long, dreary cab ride with the radio tuned to Laura Ingraham, who darkly hinted that anyone who didn't go see *Passion* was oppressing Christians.

I only read reviews of *Passion* (sorry, Laura Ingraham), but I understand most of the film amounted to watching Jesus be brutally tortured. It surprised me that Evangelicals were okay with this, because back when I was growing up they disapproved of the Catholic focus on the bloody, tortured Christ on the Cross. Not only did you not find the image of the crucified Christ in a Southern Baptist church; you didn't find a cross *at all* back then in a Southern Baptist church. I haven't been in a Southern Baptist church for a few decades, so I don't know if that's still true.

Mathewson writes that the difference between *Passion* and *Noah* goes deeper than mere biblical literacy. "The films ignite impassioned responses because they touch on an issue that lies at the very core of religious conservative piety: namely, **the distinctive understanding of the role and function of the biblical text in the formation of one's religious identity.**" (Emphasis added.)

Mathewson describes conservative Christian attitudes toward the Bible as *Biblicism*, defined as "a particular attitude of reverence for the bible as a bastion of stability amid all the fluctuation of modern life, a conscious decision to place oneself under its authority, no matter the consequences."

As I wrote earlier in this chapter, to very devout conservative Evangelicals the Bible is not just a book, and not even just a holy book. It is God's voice, perhaps even God's presence. It is not to be treated lightly. In the case of biblical films, what seems to separate what's acceptable and what isn't really doesn't have that much to do with literalism, but with reverence. You can take all kinds of liberties with the story as long as you are *worshipful* about it. And whatever you do, don't mistake God for some candy-ass liberal tree-hugger.

* * *

The issue of religious identity is one that's going to come up a few more times in the remainder of the book. By religious identity I mean merging a religious identity with the self, so that your particular sectarian niche isn't just what you believe, but who you think you are, and what you think the world is supposed to be.

A strong religious identity can override one's conscience and sweep aside doctrine, especially when threatened, because a challenge to whatever sectarian box an individual lives in feels like an existential threat to the self. Understanding this is important to understanding fanaticism and religion-associated violence, the topics of the next two chapters.

7 True Believers and Mass Movements

> Passionate hatred can give meaning and purpose to an empty life. Thus people haunted by the purposelessness of their lives try to find a new content not only by dedicating themselves to a holy cause but also by nursing a fanatical grievance. A mass movement offers them unlimited opportunities for both. — Eric Hoffer, *The True Believer: Thoughts on the Nature of Mass Movements* (1951)

Let us continue our romp through religious history, picking up where we left off in the last chapter. Here is Richard Hofstadter, from *Anti-Intellectualism in American Life,* who takes us to the aftermath of the Scopes trial and into the Franklin Roosevelt administration:

> Their heightened sense of isolation and impotence helped to bring many of the dwindling but still numerically significant fundamentalists into the ranks of a fanatical right-wing opposition to the New Deal. The fundamentalism of the cross was now supplemented by a fundamentalism of the flag. Since the 1930's, fundamentalism has been a significant component in the extreme right in American politics, whose cast of thought often shows strong fundamentalist filiations.

The cultural-religious feedback loop became a cultural-religious-political feedback loop.

> The fundamentalist mind ... is essentially Manichean; it looks upon the world as an arena for conflict between absolute good and absolute evil, and accordingly it scorns compromises (who would compromise with Satan?) and can tolerate no ambiguities. It cannot find serious importance in what it believes to be trifling degrees of difference: liberals support measures that are for all practical purposes socialistic, and socialism is nothing more than a variant of Communism, which, as everyone knows, is atheism. ... [T]he secularized fundamentalist mind begins with a definition of that which is

absolutely right, and looks upon politics as an arena in which that right must be realized.

Hofstadter published *Anti-Intellectualism in American Life* more than 50 years ago, but the paragraph above could have been written today about the Tea Party.

I wrote earlier in this book that fundamentalism isn't so much religion as it is social pathology that expresses itself as religion. Of course, religion helped create the cultural-religious-political feedback loop that fuels much of the American Right, and religion provides much of the energy that keeps it going. But my point is that when we make animus against science and rational thinking to be *just* about religion, we're missing the bigger picture.

At beginning of this chapter, I quote Eric Hoffer on the powerful combination of a holy cause and a fanatical grievance. Both of these are hallmarks of today's American religious and political Right.

Through a large part of the 20th century and going into the 21st the Right fought pitiful rearguard actions on one issue after another — opposing evolution, child labor laws, the New Deal, desegregated schools, rock 'n' roll, birth control pills, voting rights, women's liberation, gay rights — generally losing ground time after time. Legalized abortion after *Roe v. Wade* (1973) fired them up, also, although at the moment I can't say they're losing ground on abortion.

The Supreme Court decisions of the early 1960s that ended group prayers in public school classrooms also played a huge role in the increasing militancy of the religious Right. To this day the Christian Right whines about the Supreme Court kicking God out of public school. But 30 years ago Congress passed the Equal Access Act of 1984, which says that schools that allow the Girl Scouts or the school science club to meet on school property must give equal access to religion-based clubs, such as Bible study groups, as well. The U.S. Supreme Court upheld this law in *Westside School District v. Mergens* (1990). Public school students also are free to organize group prayers on public school property when they're not in class, and in public schools around the country many have done so. The only prayers that are restricted are prayers initiated by school staff (who are government employees, after all) or recited in class, in assemblies, or as part of the program at school sports events. And that's because such prayers are obvious violations of the establishment clause of the 1st Amendment to the U.S. Constitution, made applicable to states by the 14th Amendment.

(A side note: In recent years the Equal Access Act has been invoked to allow meetings of gay-straight alliances in public high schools. Irony can be fun!)

In my experience, even religious conservatives who understand that prayer and Bible study really are not banned from public school facilities still harbor a fanatical grievance about the school prayer decisions. I've come to suspect that they are too much in love with playing the role of martyr to see reason.

In *The Myth of Persecution: How Early Christians Invented a Story of Martyrdom* (HarperCollins, 2013), Candida Moss says there is little historical evidence to show that early Christians were singled out for persecution just for being Christian. In the Roman Empire people were executed in the arena for all kinds of reasons, many of which seem minor today, and Christians were executed for all kinds of reasons, too. The stories of Christians being rounded up wholesale and fed to lions merely for loving Jesus are fictions, however. Moss is a professor of New Testament and Early Christianity at the University of Notre Dame, so she would know about early Christian history more than I would.

But in her last chapter she makes a brilliant argument about how the myth of martyrdom is corroding religion and politics today. "Martyrdom is easily adapted by the powerful to cast themselves as victims," Moss writes, which justifies "their polemical and vitriolic attacks on others." Further, "members of any Christian group can claim to be persecuted as long as they feel opposed."

I'm not 100 percent persuaded that the current romance of martyrdom is just the residue of a mythical early Christian history, but the *opposition equals persecution* meme explains a lot.

Further, the sense of persecution relieves those who feel persecuted of any responsibility to reason with the opposition. If you are being persecuted, your only duty is to defend yourself by any means. You don't have to compromise, persuade or otherwise make nice.

If you pay close attention to right-wing rhetoric, you realize that the Right believes persecution authenticates their message and proves their cause is just. Moss continues,

> Similarly, in her review of David Limbaugh's book *Persecution*, Ann Coulter writes, "There is no surer proof of Christ's divinity than that he is still so hated some 2,000 years after his death." Somehow, and quite perversely, hatred has become a witness not just to truth, but to Truth. No longer are rea-

soned argument, good judgment, or logic able to win the day, because failing to convince others of one's opinions would be a better sign that one's opinions were correct. Framed by the myth that we are persecuted dialogue is not only impossible, it is undesirable. We revel in the outrage and scandal that our words and opinions elicit. We don't want to be understood by our opponent. We will fan the flames of hatred and bask in the knowledge that we are right and their criticism proves it.

As I write this, the American Christian Right is in full martyrdom mode because they are losing their campaign to deny marriage rights to same-sex couples. For example, in April 2014 the U.S. Supreme Court refused to hear a case involving a photography business penalized in state courts for refusing to photograph a lesbian wedding. Of this, Mike Huckabee — politician, radio and television personality, Baptist minister — said, "Why is it that Christians stand back and take it in the teeth time and time and time again?" In other words, not allowing Christian-owned businesses to discriminate against certain customers is the same thing as kicking all Christians in the teeth, according to Mike Huckabee. *Opposition equals oppression.*

Recently Louisiana Governor Bobby Jindal went on a tear about a "silent war" on religious liberty being waged in America by the Obama Administration and "like-minded elites" that threatens to tear the fabric of constitutional government and the fabric of communities and several other fabrics. And "It is unmistakable that most of the Obama Administration's attacks on religious liberty are aimed at conservative Christians," Gov. Jindal said.

Examples? The Governor is outraged that the Obama Administration has taken the position that private, for-profit companies cannot claim a religious exemption from including birth control coverage as part of their employee benefit packages. Also, HGTV — the HG stands for "home and garden" — dropped plans to produce a television program featuring two brothers who would have turned "fixer uppers" into dream homes. It turned out the brothers, David and Jason Benham, had a long and loud history of extremist right-wing activism, including genuinely vile hate speech aimed at homosexuals. The government had nothing to do with HGTV's dropping the program; it was a business decision. But these were the most awful examples of a "silent war" on religious liberty that Gov. Jindal could cite. *Opposition equals oppression.*

Oh, but it gets *so* much better. Rep. Louie Gohmert (R-TX) was also outraged by the cancelation of the Benham twins' program. "We see these kinds of receptions for conservatives, for Judeo-Christian believers and followers, people eliminated from being on television because they hold the view espoused by Moses and by Jesus of marriage being between a man and a woman," Gohmert said. I'd always thought Moses was a polygamist with two wives, but I checked, and apparently the Bible is ambiguous about the wives.

Anyway, Rep. Gohmert went on to call the courts' striking down of same-sex marriage bans as "fascist intolerance." The legalization of same-sex marriage and the cancellation of the Benham twins' program are *just like Nazi Germany*, Rep. Gohmert said, and *just as bad* as female genital mutilation. *Opposition equals oppression.*

The golden age of biblical epic films may be over, but the golden age of Christian persecution films may have just begun. Eric Brown of the *International Business Times* reported that an independent film titled *God's Not Dead* had grossed more than $34 million in its first three weeks in theaters. Moviefone reported that the indie film was the fifth highest-earning film on the weekend it opened, in March 2014.[xxxi] The highly promoted *Divergent* and *Muppets Most Wanted* were among its competition.

The film, which I have not seen, depicts a college student whose philosophy professor demands the class write "God is dead" on a piece of paper, sign it, and hand it in. The student, a Christian, refuses. I assume several other things happen to fill the film's running time. Eric Brown writes,

> Russell Wolfe, CEO of "God's Not Dead" distributor Pure Flix, admitted in an interview with the Blaze, the Glenn Beck site, that the film is, by and large, 'preaching to the choir,' saying that 'God's Not Dead' helps 'people know more of why they believe what they believe.' But what values is the film teaching? Between the film's abusive Muslims and angry atheists, the biggest take-home is that everyone is out to get Christians. [xxxii]

I read that not just one, but two indie Christian persecution films are scheduled for release later in 2014, both named *Persecuted*. This is from a press release about one of them:

> PERSECUTED tells the story of a modern-day evangelist named John Luther, played by SAG Award-nominated and

Saturn Award winning actor James Remar (X-MEN: FIRST CLASS, 'Dexter', DJANGO: UNCHAINED, WHAT LIES BENEATH, RED). Luther is the last hold out for a national endorsement to make sweeping reform in freedom of speech. As the government is mandating political correctness while covertly waging a war against religious organizations, a U.S. Senator, portrayed by Oscar-nominated actor Bruce Davison (X-MEN, 'Lost', 'Castle'), and his political allies create a sinister plan of denial and scandal to frame John Luther for murder. Suddenly his once normal life is turned upside down as he becomes a fugitive vowing to expose those responsible. It is a mission that brings him face-to-face with the coming storm of persecution that will threaten the moral ethics and freedoms of America.

Since "mandating political correctness" usually means being slammed for tweeting racist jokes involving black people and watermelons, I attempted to find out what awful thing is being mandated in the film. It appears to be a hypothetical "Faith and Fairness Act" that would require religious broadcasters to present all religious points of view when presenting their own point of view. Well, yes, that would be dreadful. I shudder at the thought of anyone on the Christian Broadcasting Network attempting to present a Buddhist point of view. Please, don't.

The other *Persecuted* is set in the old Soviet Union and involves Evangelicals being pursued by KGB agents, but Miranda Blue at Right Wing Watch says the film is "clearly meant to be an allegorical tale about the United States today." [xxxiii] As it hasn't been released as of this writing, I can't say that's true. We'll see.

But if that's not enough Christian persecution porn for you, a "Stories of the Persecuted Church" boxed set of six *more* Christian persecution films on DVD is available from ChristianCinema.com.

In some parts of the world Christians really are subject to genuine persecution, as are people of other religions. And in some parts of the world Christians have done and are doing the persecuting — Christians are behind Uganda's notorious anti-gay laws, for example.[xxxiv] But within the United States, however much Christians may want to wallow in martyrdom, they are only being persecuted in their own fantasies. Seriously, do we want to talk about the annual War on Christmas, in which conservative media personalities blather incessantly about the persecution of Christians because department store clerks wish them "Happy Holidays" instead of "Merry Christmas"?

Holy cause, check. Fanatical grievance, check.

* * *

We learned in the 20th century that destructive mass movements don't need religion to become powerful. The spread of fascism in Europe and the totalitarian regimes of Mao Zedong and Joseph Stalin were able to manipulate public opinion and take and maintain power, for example, without appeals to religion, and even while being openly atheistic.

However, a number of bright people have argued that religion prepared the ground for these totalitarian regimes, so religion is still to blame for them even if the movement's leaders promoted atheism.

Here's the theory: Authoritarian mass movements tend to promote something like a messianic worldview; a belief that current struggles and hardships will establish a worker's paradise, or put German-speaking white people in charge of everything, or some such.

The argument, then, is that generations of messianic theology instilled a deep belief that history has some pre-ordained arc toward utopian perfection. This messianic thinking can morph into beliefs about an impossibly perfect political or national destiny, which then fuel fanaticism and war as the true believers strive to achieve it.

This is a *very* compelling argument. I even can think of a more recent example of messianic thinking causing big trouble. Back in 1989 an American political scientist named Francis Fukuyama published an essay called "The End of History," which then morphed into a book called *The End of History and the Last Man*.[xxxv] And for years I kept seeing references to Fukayama's "end of history" argument that praised it as maybe the pinnacle of western philosophical thought. Fukayama was particularly popular among the neoconservatives, whom you might remember as the faction most gung-ho for the U.S. to invade Iraq in 2003.

Every time I heard about the "end of history" I assumed the title was metaphorical and represented some sophisticated and subtle reasoning that would go over my head. But I finally got my hands on the original essay, and read it, and realized with growing horror that the title was *literal*. Fukayama believed that the collapse of the Soviet Union proved that someday the whole world, or most of it anyway, would be ruled by western-style democracy and capitalism, and when this happened it would be the end point of human cultural and social evolution. As a species, we will have arrived at our glorious, ultimate destiny, as all governments would be western-style democracies and all people would be rewarded with the blessings of capitalism and live happily ever after.

I learned later that I wasn't the only one who thought this bit of sophistry was warmed-over Christian eschatology; the Second Coming minus Jesus. But I could see why the neocons loved it. Neocons are, basically, pro-active American isolationists who want to make the globe a less foreign and more America-like place by spreading American hegemony (and capitalism!), by force if need be. This is for everyone's own good, of course. Fukayama's essay became scripture that supported their "religious" views.

To one degree or another, messianic theology is wired into the religions that originated in Persia and Mesopotamia — the Abrahamic religions, Zoroastrianism, and so on. However, I'm not aware of messianic thought in the traditions that emerged from the Vedic religions of India, and the connection between messianic thought and the indigenous Chinese religions, Daoism and Confucianism, is murky. So the rise of Mao Zedong seems not so connected to messianic theology. On the other hand, the cult of Mao no doubt *did* take advantage of traditional Chinese belief in the emperor as the "son of heaven" and something of a divine figure.

However, we may be mistaking effect for cause. Maybe, a need to believe in a pre-ordained arc toward utopian perfection, or a great and enduring destiny that will emerge from current struggles, or a Big Daddy leader figure in general, is wired into us at a more primordial level than religious belief.

Sigmund Freud thought that the human need for religion is an echo of our helplessness as an infant and the desire to be protected by a parental figure. But might that not also apply to authoritarian mass movements that are not religious? It's perhaps the case that messianic theology and messianic politics both arise from the same deeply ingrained psychological impulse, rather than one causing the other. What we really want is a big adult person who will love us and protect us and fix our broken toys and make everything better. That wouldn't *have* to be God, you know.

And especially in times of great social change or insecurity, we may tell ourselves that our current struggles are going to lead to a glorious resolution, if only to keep from falling into fear and despair.

* * *

Instead of reflexively blaming religion for everything that goes wrong in the world, I think it's more useful to consider the complex social and psychological reasons people get sucked into authoritarian mass movements, or cling to irrational beliefs, whether religious or non-religious.

In the 20th century some very smart people wrote about this. One of these was Eric Hoffer (1902-1983), whose book *The True Believer: Thoughts on the Nature of Mass Movements* (1951) ought to be required reading for all sentient beings. I quote Hoffer at the beginning of this chapter.

Another was Erich Fromm (1900-1980), a psychoanalyst, sociologist, and philosopher who also studied the Talmud as a young man. He escaped from Nazi Germany and went on to write extensively about the rise of authoritarian mass movements and the psychological reasons people join them. Fromm published several good books, beginning with *Escape From Freedom* (1941).

Both Fromm and Hoffer recognized that people march blindly into mass movements because the movement provides something the individual feels is lacking in himself. By submerging individual identity with the group, the helpless can feel powerful, the wronged can be validated, and the confused can find certitude.

In *Escape From Freedom*, Fromm said that while people want freedom in the abstract, when they actually have it they can find it isolating and bewildering. Like Freud, Fromm was a psychoanalyst — although he didn't always agree with Freud — and he looked deeply at humans as creatures of culture and society and also at the irrational and subconscious forces that drive us.

Among other things, we humans have a deep need to *belong*. We need to feel that our lives have some significance in the great scheme of things. We need to feel we have a secure position within our in-the-flesh social network. We need to feel related to the world, somehow. And we will grasp desperately at just about anything that will give us what we need to feel.

"Religion and nationalism," Fromm wrote, "as well as any custom and any belief however absurd and degrading, if it only connects the individual with others, are refuges from what man most dreads: isolation."

Further,

[M]an, the more he gains freedom in the sense of emerging from the original oneness with man and nature and the more he becomes an "individual," has no choice but to unite himself with the world in the spontaneity of love and productive work, or else to seek a kind of security by such ties with the world as destroy his freedom and the integrity of his individual self.

Fromm's essential message was that those who fear personal freedom, who are uncomfortable with their own autonomy, will "escape" freedom by plunging into authoritarian movements and/or conformity.

* * *

Another way to put this is that we humans tend to join tribes. A tribe in this sense is an association with an institution or other group of people that your ego attaches to; that you adopt as part of your own self-identity. So, when your tribe is threatened, particularly by another tribe, the ego reacts as if the self is threatened.

Tribes can be ethnic or religious, and they can also be ideological or political. Even with ideological and political tribes, loyalty to the tribe and its tenets becomes more important than logic, reason, real-world events, the normal functions of government, or even individual self-interest. One is loyal, *because*. People outside the tribe are either dupes or the enemy, *because*.

Logical reasons backed by empirical data are never given; if you try to discuss their opinions with them, the loyal tribal member just repeats the approved tribal talking points as the received wisdom of the tribe. That is all one needs to know.

One of the terrible ironies of current American political culture is that it is largely populated by tribes of people who fancy themselves as *freedom* fighters as they march in mindless ideological lockstep, from gun-toting right-wing "patriots" to libertarians clinging to their zombie ideas about free-market economics.[xxxvi] My personal favorites are the "objectivists," a tribe of Ayn Rand disciples who claim to be opposed to tribes, all mechanically quoting the same passages from *Atlas Shrugged* to show how individual they are.

Tribes can be based on fanatic devotion to ideologies, and sometimes they're collective fantasies that people escape into. Or both.

And yes, I see examples of tribalism on the Left as well. U.S. lefties can get very tribal over potential Democratic presidential candidates, for example. The 2008 Hillary Clinton-Barack Obama contest had many former activist allies at each other's throats, which was odd considering the two candidates had nearly identical stands on most issues. I am not look-ing forward to 2016.

On the Right, much tribalism in the U.S. currently is being manip-ulated by special interests with deep pockets. Climate change denialism is being sponsored with "dark money" that appears to come from the petro-leum industry, for example.[xxxvii] Left-wing tribalism in the U.S. is not nearly so well funded or well organized.

For many people the world is a much more precarious place to live than it was 40 years ago. Job and financial security have seriously eroded, for example. Community and family life have broken up for many. And, frankly, increasing racial and religious diversity is not sitting well with some folks. Overwhelmed with existential angst, many are seeking a kind of security by such ties with the world as destroy their freedom and the integrity of their individual selves. And sometimes they do this wearing tri-corner hats and waving "don't tread on me" signs.

My point here is that it is absurd to point to *religion* as the sole source of the irrationality of public life. I sincerely believe that if religion disappeared tomorrow, all the tribalism, bigotry, and fear fueling the cha-os would just find another container. A lot of it already has.

*   *   *

I've been talking throughout this book of the importance of feeling connected to *something* beyond the limited self. How is that different from joining a cult?

I've also been stressing the word *intimacy*. The spiritual quest needs to be grounded in deep intimacy, deep self-awareness and self-honesty. The spiritual practitioner must strive to own up to his own crazi-ness and whatever ugly, dark things inhabit his subconscious. He must come to terms with the causes and conditions that fuel him — what he wants, why he wants it.

This is not exactly confessing sins, although confessing sins might be part of it. It's also acknowledging wounds, resentments, bitterness, dis-appointments and unhappiness generally. It's being able to recognize when we're playing the martyr, victim, hero, or drama queen, and *stop*.

The mystical tradition of Christianity, according to the written rec-ords of the mystics, was based on deep contemplation. They did not look for God up in the sky but within their own hearts. Saint Augustine said, "Do not go outward; return within yourself. In the inward person dwells truth." Likewise, the older mystical traditions of Asia nearly all emphasize some kind of contemplative meditation.

Mysticism tends to be full of paradoxes, and the chief paradox may be that the path to transcending the limited self goes *through* the self, not away from it.

Here's a little more from Eric Hoffer:

> Only the individual who has come to terms with his self can have a dispassionate attitude toward the world. Once the harmony with the self is upset, he turns into a highly reactive entity. Like an unstable chemical radical he hungers to combine with whatever comes within his reach. He cannot stand apart, whole or self-sufficient, but has to attach himself whole-heartedly to one side or the other.

Self-intimacy, self-awareness, is what makes the difference between connection with the cosmos or connection with a cult. And this is huge. I can't stress enough how important this is.

* * *

> The hand pointing to the moon is not the moon. — old Zen saying

* * *

You can think of a belief system or ideology, whether religious, philosophical or political, as just an interface between you and reality. As a Zen student that's not *exactly* how I see ideologies, but for now I think it's a workable conceptual model.

The interface is not reality itself. It's a contrivance that sorts phenomena into categories and provides basic explanations for why things are the way things are, to make reality easier to understand. We all carry such contrived systems in our heads, to one extent or another, even if we don't think of ourselves as "believers."

Some very basic belief systems have been programmed into us from birth by our families and cultures, for example. And if everyone we know sorts, labels and understands reality the same way we do, we don't recognize this as programming; we think it's just "common sense." It usually takes an extraordinary experience or circumstance for someone to recognize primary programming as programming.

Most of the time, though, when we're talking about an ideology or a belief system we're talking about some mode of understanding that we have adopted because we think it "makes sense," which usually means it conforms to our biases.

I do like to think some portion of humanity really does consider real-world evidence and come to rational conclusions about things, of course, but it's rare, and no one is completely free of programming.

Because "reality" is infinitely complicated, we all rely on interfaces of some sort to navigate it. But no belief system or ideology is ever 100 percent correct. Some of them can be reasonably accurate in some ways, but you're always going to bump into situations the interface wasn't designed to handle. As long as we understand that our belief systems and ideologies are not reality itself, however, we can take note of discrepancies and *adjust*. We can update the interface in light of new knowledge and experience. This is the rational thing to do.

But that's unusual. Most people do confuse the interface between themselves and reality with reality itself. And most of us set up elaborate filtering systems in our heads to *protect the interface*. When confronted with data that our interface can't process, most of us will distort the data to make it "work" with the interface or dismiss it as an aberration. Even well-educated and intelligent people do this.

And then there are politicians. Political beliefs and opinions are interfaces. They are never reality itself. In politics, an "ideologue" is not just someone who holds an ideology of some sort, because that would make all of us ideologues. An ideologue is, instead, someone who values the ideology above all things. Maintaining the integrity of the ideology and being loyal to its tenets are more important, to an ideologue, than are the real-world results of enacting the ideology.

Just one random example — in 2010 Texas Governor Rick Perry was interviewed by Evan Smith, editor of the *Texas Tribune*. Smith asked the Governor about sex education in Texas public schools. "Governor, why does Texas continue with abstinence education programs when they don't seem to be working?" Smith questioned. "In fact, we have the third-highest teen pregnancy rate in the country, among all the states."

"Abstinence works," the Governor replied.

Smith, somewhat exasperated, pushed the question again — according to statistics, Smith said, it's not working at all. Could the Governor provide some data to show that it *is* working? But the Governor simply replied that abstinence-only was the best way to teach sex education. And when Smith pushed the question again, the irritated Governor said that he knew abstinence works "from personal experience," a line that inspired much giggling among bloggers. Governor Perry added that he wasn't about "to stand up here and say, 'Y'all go have sex and have the whatever is going on.'"[xxxviii]

I interpret the Governor's remarks to be that abstinence-only education "works" in the sense that it conforms to conservative principles. Whether it actually stops the young folks from making babies and spreading STDs is beside the point.

* * *

I began the first chapter of this book with a quotation from Sigmund Freud, who called attempts to defend religion from modern rational thought a "pitiful rearguard action." I think the "rearguard action" is exactly that, but it's not just about religion. I think most of it is a reactionary effort to delay a future in which national, racial, cultural, and ethnic boundaries have blurred. And it's a future in which once-dominant factions will lose their power to shame and oppress others into submission. They fear that someday the last really will be first and they, who feel entitled to be first, will be last.[xxxix]

But these days even bigots recognize, however dimly, that bigotry is *bad*. So they dress it up as religion, because if their biases are somehow dictated by faith, they are (in their minds) sanctified and untouchable. So you end up with a Bizarro World religion in which, for example, not being allowed to discriminate against gays is religious persecution.

Late in 2013, frenzy erupted over remarks made by Phil Robertson, one of the subjects of the "reality" television program *Duck Dynasty*. Robertson likened homosexual sex to bestiality and terrorism. He also suggested that all non-Christians are terrorists and murderers and that African Americans were happier under Jim Crow laws than they are now.

According to the Right, Robertson was only expressing what the Bible said about homosexuality. (They carefully avoided dealing with the "non-Christians are terrorists" and Jim Crow remarks.) Further, he had added the qualifier that it was not for him to judge. See? He's not a bad guy.

This is a cheap hatemonger's trick; say hateful things and then add the qualifier "but it's not up to me to judge." Or worse, there's the even more phony "hate the sin but love the sinner," usually added after some horrendously hateful speech about the "sinner." Such qualifiers are supposed to cancel out the ugly thing that was just said. This is a variation of the "I was just joking" qualifier that's supposed to make it okay to wish someone would eat poison and die.[xl]

Rule: If you say something bigoted and hateful, you don't get to deflect criticism by hiding behind the Bible. People who object to this rule might want to consult Matthew 15:11.[xli]

In the next chapter, on Religion and Violence, I'm going to say more about using religion as a moral cover for bad behavior. I think most of the time religion is not so much the cause as the excuse. Sometimes it's a post-hoc excuse, trotted out after a speaker realizes he's gone too far. Sometimes it's a permission slip a speaker gives himself because he sees himself as one of the *good guys*, so anything he says must be righteous.

This brings us to the topic of personal narratives and myths.

* * *

Those who totally realize delusion are buddhas. Those who are totally deluded about realization are ordinary people. [Eihei Dogen, "Genjokoan" (1233)] [xlii]

* * *

People believe all kinds of unmitigated nonsense that doesn't have anything to do with religion. We humans, religious and not, will believe things without evidence, or with much-debunked evidence — that vaccines cause autism, for example — probably because *we really want to believe them.*

As an eyewitness to the collapse of the World Trade Center towers I find 9/11 truthers particularly irritating. But the truther phenomenon begs a huge question — why do people *want* to believe this? What is it in their psychological makeup that makes nonsensical stories about secret controlled demolitions and holographic jet planes so compelling to them? Richard Hofstadter, writing in the 1950s and 1960s, described similar conspiracy theory cults throughout American history, so it's hardly an isolated phenomenon.

We all tend to believe things we want to believe. We easily believe nasty rumors about people we don't like, for example. It takes a certain amount of maturity and self-awareness to acknowledge that something we *really want* to believe might not be true. I suppose some of us are deficient in self-awareness filters.

In his book *The Unpersuadables*, which really is the best thing I've read on this topic, Will Storr suggests that our thinking skills haven't evolved beyond the age of myth as much as we think. Our brains are wired to look for connections and meaning, and so we see connections and meaning whether they are there or not. Our experiences are framed by our personal, mythical (and usually self-flattering) narratives, not data. We feel emotions and impulses, generated in the subconscious, that we cannot explain, so we make up stories to explain them. We create our stories from our biases, however, not from objective fact, and that's how we interpret the world. *And we all do this*, religious or not.

Indeed, it may be that the most foolish belief of all is the belief that any of us are rational. The only difference between a sensible person and a kook may be that the sensible person holds irrational beliefs that conform to a socially acceptable norm, while the kook is more creative.

I would argue that some of us do critically examine what we want to believe, though, at least some of the time. We may hear a rumor about X, and we may want to believe it, and we may flirt with believing it. But then we cast about for something approximating objective fact to support X, and if we don't find it we reluctantly put X aside, clinging to a hope that maybe it's true while acknowledging that it possibly isn't. However, if X is something that can't be objectively verified, one way or another, we'll likely go along with whatever most of our peers believe about it.

Others of us, apparently, have no self-critical filters at all and embrace whatever we want to believe as the Holy Truth. And if you can find fellow travelers who have embraced the same beliefs you've got yourself a mass movement, or at least a Band of Feedback Loopy Brothers.

As I write this there are some would-be warriors camped on the Nevada desert in the belief that they are at war with the U.S. departments of Justice and the Interior, Bureau of Land Management (BLM). In brief, a Nevada rancher had refused to pay lawful grazing fees for his cattle to graze on public land for more than 20 years and owed the federal government more than a million dollars in fees and fines. And after more than 20 years of warnings, legal actions and court judgments against the rancher, in April 2014 the BLM attempted to remove and confiscate the trespassing cattle. But the BLM agents soon were facing a few hundred heavily armed men who had gathered to defend the rancher from "government overreach," which is how the self-appointed militia viewed the BLM's attempt to enforce the law. The BLM withdrew.

This situation could still end in violence and tragedy, but at the moment it cries out to be immortalized in film by Christopher Guest. Several days have passed and some of the militia have not gone home. One group, citing "intel" that the United States Attorney General had ordered a drone strike to take them out, redeployed to a motel. Another group remained in their camp, calling the first group cowards and traitors who probably had been working for the government all along. The second group apparently believes the drone strike threat also, and in their videos they have taken to calling their camp the "kill zone."

Their videos also feature talk of the "command structure," the "field of battle" and "the enemy," by which they appear to mean the United States government. In a real dictatorship they would have disappeared days ago.

And for all the world they resemble little boys who have made a backyard fort out of cardboard boxes, stocked it with Oreos and toy guns and remain inside, vigilant for enemy squirrels or worse, *their sisters*. But these are large adult men with real assault weapons who honestly believe they are the last holdouts of freedom against a tyrannical government. This may not end well.

* * *

"The scientific method is the tool that humans have developed to break the dominion of the narrative," Will Storr writes. I have the modern person's standard trust in science, and I don't think that trust is misplaced. Science has given us wonderful technology, advances in medicine, better understanding of the nature of life forms and the cosmos. If a majority of scientists decide X is Y I tend to believe them and trust they've got the data, somewhere, to back it up. Scientists make mistakes, and bias does creep into results sometimes, but the scientific method itself has a proven track record of getting at the facts of things eventually.

Science begat scientism, however. Scientism is the belief that science is the only source of truth and has the power to unlock all mysteries of any sort. Conversely, anything that science cannot know isn't "real," anyway.

Life and consciousness may be mysteries, but I've met people who are certain science is on the verge of creating life and synthesizing consciousness. And the "fact" that science is about to do this is presented as evidence that religion can't claim anything is mysterious. I can understand why someone who has issues with religion would want to believe this, since many religion apologists do like their "god of the gaps" arguments.

Maybe science will create life and consciousness some day, but the claims of "creating life" most recently are based on research that injects synthetic DNA into living microbes. As I understand it, synthetic DNA strands can be created by computer and made usable by being soaked in a yeast culture. Then the synthesized DNA is inserted into microbes that adapt to the new genetic coding. I may be getting that wrong, but that's how the process has been explained in news stories.

This is very exciting stuff, but that doesn't sound like "creating" life to me. It sounds more like "adapting" life. And artificial consciousness is still on the drawing board, as far as I can tell. Researchers are struggling just to define consciousness, artificial or otherwise.

I say scientism is unscientific, because it proposes something — that there is no sort of truth that can't be revealed through the scientific method — that cannot be verified through the scientific method. It's something that has to be accepted on faith. True believers of scientism have an absolute snit when you tell them that, though.

What's happening with scientism believers (scientismists?), seems to me, is that they very much *want* to believe they are as entirely rational as computers and utterly unlike those irrational religion-believing people they so dislike. So the myth-making parts of their brains have developed a strong cognitive bias to "confirm" their belief in absolute rationality and of themselves as relentlessly rational. They're living in a myth that they're not living in a myth.

I say a person cannot be genuinely rational until he recognizes and acknowledges his own irrationality. Otherwise, he's just kidding himself.

* * *

The proposition that we're all living in our own myth explains a lot.

For example, I grew up in an all-white small town in the 1950s, where white racism and even white supremacism weren't that unusual. I noticed years ago that hard-core white supremacists often are the most average people you can imagine. Most of the time they aren't particularly smart, or particularly handsome, or particularly accomplished, or particularly talented, or particularly successful, or particularly anything. The only thing they've got going for themselves is being white.

So they live inside a myth that being white makes them really, really special, but there are Evil Dark or Liberal Beings out there who hate them and want to oppress them for their specialness. Seriously; if you actually listen to their rhetoric what's often striking is that they sound almost jealous of racial minorities for getting more sympathy and attention than they do. So in their minds they've got themselves a holy cause and a whiz-bang fanatical grievance. There are exceptions to everything, but I'd bet that my hypothesis accounts for most of them.

I also have met progressive activists who get a little too caught up in their personal myths of being The People's Crusaders. For example, there's a class of them I call "vocational protesters," because they've shown up in force at every rally or march I've ever attended. However, this crew often behaves in a way that is detrimental to the Cause, whatever it is, such as carrying inappropriate signs or wearing goofy or vulgar costumes. And then they complain that "the man" doesn't take them seriously.

Along with the costumes, people show up with megaphones at what are supposed to be silent protests and piggy-back all kinds of unrelated causes onto what the rally or march is supposed to be about. In other words, they appear to view demonstrations as opportunities for self-expression — and acting out their personal myths — rather than as means to join with others to affect political change.

I confess I can't quite put my finger on what myth 9/11 truthers are living in, though. It appears to be a sort of holy crusader myth, but why it's so important for them to believe the terrorist attacks were an "inside job" I have no idea.

In centuries past, people with a psychological need to believe in a vast evil conspiracy could always turn to the demonic beliefs of religion. Why anyone would have such a need I do not know, but it seems to be a common syndrome. In more modern times, however, there are many other kinds of threatening super powers and demonic minions to choose from. What with the global reach of governments, secret surveillance watching us through our smart phones, evil "vampire squid" multinational corporations, terrorist networks and sleeper cells, black ops and black sites, and so on, the old God vs. Lucifer face-off seems rather boring, somehow. You don't hear much about alien abductions these days, either.

Humanity has finally become its own monster-under-the-bed.

8 Religion and Violence

Fear is born from arming oneself. — The Buddha, Attadanda
Sutta [xliii]

Right now in Burma (also called Myanmar) Buddhists have taken to violently attacking Muslims, and their argument is that it's justified because they are "defending Buddhism." But the Buddha was even more uncompromising about not hating and not committing violence than Jesus was, so they are violating the religion they say they are defending.

I say this is a variation of destroying a village to save it.

From what I can tell from the other side of the world, racism and nationalism are fueling the violence as much as religious fervor. I've read analyses of the situation in Burma saying that reactionary factions in the government are using reactionary monks for their own ends. Of course, maybe the monks are using the politicians for *their* own ends.

According to Kyaw San Wai of the S. Rajaratnam School of International Studies (RSIS) in Singapore, another factor is "a long standing siege mentality of the Burmese populace drawing on Buddhist millenarianism and a sense of demographic besiegement."[xliv] Note that millenarianism is not compatible with formal Buddhist doctrine, although millenarian-Buddhist cults have cropped up in Asian history from time to time.

Kyaw San Wai explains,

> Among Burmese Buddhists, there is a widespread belief that Buddhism will disappear in the future. While international coverage points to Myanmar's religious demographics to discredit fears of Islamic encroachment, Burmese Buddhists have a starkly different world view where their faith is besieged by larger, well-endowed and better-organised faiths. This millenarianism can be traced to a scripturally unsupported but widely believed "prophecy" that Buddhism will disappear 5000 years after the Buddha's passing. As 1956 is considered the halfway point, the belief is that Buddhism is now declining irreversibly.

The residue of British colonialism is also fueling a sense of be-siegement, Kyaw San Wai says. A series of Anglo-Burmese wars resulted in Burma being annexed into the British Raj in 1886. British management of Burma dismantled traditional Burmese social structures and also opened the country to a torrent of Christian missionaries and non-Burmese mi-grant laborers from India, which fed the above-mentioned millenarianism. A rebellion, joined at times by Buddhist monks, pushed back against the British in 1936 and 1937 but was put down forcefully by British police, in some cases by firing into crowds and killing unarmed protesters.

Burma gained its independence only after Britain lost control of India in 1947. But by then Burma could not be put back together the way it was before colonialism.

Most Burmese Muslims belong to an ethnic group called the Rohingya, who live mostly in a section of western Burma bordering the Bay of Bengal and Bangladesh. Rohingya had settled there in the 15th cen-tury, possibly earlier, but in the 18th century political upheavals caused them to flee to Bangladesh. In the 19th, century, after the British takeover, the British encouraged the Rohingya to return to their former lands in Burma.

After Burma became independent in 1947, the Rohingya Muslims were considered to be citizens and allowed to vote. But a military coup d'état in 1962 changed everything in Burma, and not for the better. Among other things, the military junta ruling Burma stripped the Rohingya of citi-zenship and denied them basic rights. Rohingya sometimes were scape-goated by the junta to deflect attention from the junta's own misconduct. On several occasions Rohingya fled into Bangladesh seeking safety, but Bangladesh refused to give them refugee status and forced them back to Burma.

Meanwhile, the Buddhist population of Burma suffered terrible hardships because of the junta's corruption and mismanagement. Some desperate families gave their young sons to the monasteries, to be raised as monks, so at least the boys would have food and shelter. This has resulted, I'm told, in a population of monks with *issues* and more interest in politics than in dharma.

In 2008, under international pressure, Burma adopted a new con-stitution that required a return to elected government. The first elections, in 2010, were widely regarded as fixed. Elections held in April 2012 elect-ed a slate of reformers to Parliament, however, including Nobel Peace Prize laureate Aung San Suu Kyi. Hold that thought.

The current violence began in August 2012, when a Buddhist woman of western Burma was found raped and murdered. Rohingyas were blamed — I don't believe the perpetrator was ever identified — and mob violence began. Since then there have been recurring waves of mob violence, and by many accounts some have been as brutal as mob violence gets. As of April 2014 more than 300 people have been killed, most of them Rohingya Muslims.

A faction of Buddhist monks led by a monk named Wirathu has spoken in favor of the oppression of the Rohingya, being careful to stop just short of explicitly advocating murder. Wirathu also produces anti-Muslim DVDs and uses social media to spread rumors against Muslims.

People close to this situation report tacit co-operation in tactics and rhetoric between anti-reform government hard-liners and the monks. It's widely suggested that the violence is being used to put the brakes on government reform.

It has also been suggested that the political hard-liners, who seriously hate Aung San Suu Kyi, orchestrated the violence to force her into a trap — either side with the Muslims and lose the next election, or side with the Buddhists and lose the support of the international community. One Burma observer, former U.S. Congressman Tom Andrews (D-Maine) — who today leads Win Without War, chairs the Council for a Livable World's PeacePAC and is a board member of the U.S. foreign policy reform group Just Foreign Policy — said that in Burma "Muslims are the third rail of politics. No politician in Burma can make a stand for a reviled minority and still be elected."[xlv]

Aung San Suu Kyi has attempted to remain vague, thereby pissing off just about everybody.

At the same time, other Burmese monks *have* spoken out against Wirathu and the violence, and in 2013 one Buddhist monastery opened its doors to Muslims fleeing the mobs, offering them food and shelter. My understanding is that the hate-mongering monks are a minority faction and not representative of Burma's monastic *sangha*. However, Buddhist monastic tradition long has been a bit fuzzy about ecclesiastical authority, and it appears there is no single Buddhist authority in Burma that could compel Wirathu and the hate mongers to stand down.

The newest wrinkle as of this writing is that the hate-mongering monks have formed a new group called Organization for the Protection of Race, Religion, and Belief. Assuming the translation is accurate, notice that race is listed first.

Burma is about 90 percent Buddhist and 4 to 8 percent Muslim, which makes the notion that Muslims are somehow taking over in Burma irrational on its face. Yet that's what I've been hearing from some Burmese Buddhists.

When I've criticized the violence on the Web I am told I don't understand how dangerous radical Islam can be. Did I mention I was in lower Manhattan on September 11, 2001? That I'm an eyewitness to the collapse of the World Trade Center towers? I believe I do understand. But I also understand that bigotry is bigotry. And you don't appease hate with more hate.

The Buddha said exactly that, by the way — "Hatred is not appeased by hatred. By non-hatred alone is hatred appeased. This is a law eternal." See the Dhammapada, verse 5.

* * *

My account of the situation in Burma barely scratches the surface of what's going on there. And please note that I have no firsthand information, and my analysis may be inaccurate. However, I chose the Burmese situation to illustrate religious violence because it's a relatively straightforward example, and I thought in the interest of fairness I might as well call out my own "team" and not pick on someone else's. In fact, I'm going to focus mostly on Buddhism for examples of religious violence just to keep the chapter manageable, but I believe my examples are representative of most religious violence.

Let's consider where is this violence coming from, and whether Buddhism or something else is primarily to blame. For example, what justifications might be found for anti-Muslim or other violence in Buddhist scripture?

Burma's monks are of the Theravada tradition, and as I explained in the chapter on scripture, the sole Theravada scriptural canon is the Pali Tipitika or Pali Canon. I do not have an exhaustive knowledge of the Pali Canon, but those who do say there is absolutely no justification in it for the violence in Burma.

Although Buddhism has never been absolutely pacifistic, there is no Buddhist "just war" theory, according to Theravadin monk, scholar and translator Thanissaro Bhikkhu.[xlvi] A follower of the Buddha *may* blamelessly defend himself from violence in some circumstances, but only if the self-defending is done without malice toward the attacker and with no desire for revenge. To initiate violence for any reason is a violation of the teachings. A follower of the Buddha may not even harbor ill will toward another being, even if he doesn't act on it, without creating all kinds of really unfortunate karma. These teachings clearly are stated and re-stated in many places in the Pali Tipitika.

Buddhist morality also flows from practice of the *Brahma-vihara*, which is a list of four "immeasurable" virtues to be cultivated by a follower of the Buddha. These are *metta* (loving kindness for all beings, without exception), *karuna* (compassion, also for all beings), *mudita* (empathy, or more literally "sympathetic joy," or joy for the good fortune of others) and *upekkha* (equanimity, which has many facets, including not being drawn into taking sides in partisan conflicts). I confess I could do with more cultivating myself. The point is, though, that these are very basic teachings that even a novice monk would know by heart.

The belief in a time when the Buddha's teachings will be forgotten, which may be fueling Burmese violence, *is* widespread in Buddhism. In fact, it's part of a recurring pattern. Buddhist scriptures say there were some number of Buddhas before ours, and whenever the dharma is forgotten a new Buddha comes to teach it just as it was taught before. And then some measure of time later it is forgotten again. As in Hinduism, in Buddhism the ages of the cosmos are thought to come and go in an endless cycle rather than build toward a glorious, utopian future.

The only Theravada scripture I know of that gives a timeline for future decline of the teaching is the Pali Vinaya-pitaka's story of the first ordination of women as nuns. The Buddha is quoted as saying that if women were ordained his teachings would survive only five hundred years. And if he said that he was wrong, since he ordained women, anyway, and that was way more than five hundred years ago. But this story does not appear in the corresponding Sanskrit/Chinese Vinaya, which suggests that it was added to the Pali scriptures *later*.

Further, in most schools of Buddhism the great sages have taught that linear time is an illusion. This would throw the "prophecy" into the realm of allegory, and not something to be believed in literally.

* * *

It used to be claimed in the West that no wars were ever fought in the name of Buddhism, although I haven't heard that one lately. It's true — at least, I'm reasonably certain it's true — there is no Buddhist equivalent of the Crusades, and no example of warfare to conquer non-Buddhist people to force them to convert. However, wars have been fought *over* Buddhism, in one way or another.

One of the more clear-cut examples occurred in the 17th century, when Mongol and Tibetan troops, on the orders of His Holiness the 5th Dalai Lama, attacked an encampment of monks of the Kagyu school, headed by His Holiness the 10th Karmapa. The 5th Dalai Lama had just assumed rule of Tibet, and the 10th Karmapa would not agree to accept his authority. Several monks were killed in the attack, and His Holiness the 10th Karmapa fled into exile to the mountains of Bhutan.

The two holinesses have since patched things up. Currently the 14th Dalai Lama is mentoring the much younger 17th Karmapa, or at least one of the 17th Karmapas, as the Kagyu school currently is split over the identity of the 17th Karmapa.

Sometimes Buddhist clergy have gotten mixed up in other people's political wars. There is archeological evidence that in the early 7th century, kung fu-master Chan monks from the famous Shaolin Temple of China took part in battles that helped establish the Tang Dynasty. In the 16th century the Shaolin monks were called upon to defend the coast of China from Japanese pirates, which sounds to me like the synopsis of a great martial arts movie.

Throughout Asia it was common for monasteries to have some "warrior monks" trained and ready to defend the monastery from bandits or other aggressors. And occasionally the warrior monks got a tad proactive and got into fights with another monastery's warrior monks.

So, bottom line, there have been times in which Buddhist clergy and institutions have supported and taken part in some kind of violence or warfare. More often than not, these episodes were connected to political power, either their own or that of a patron warlord or king.

Such patronage wasn't taken for granted. Several times in Asian history when Buddhist monks and nuns lost the favor of a monarch, their monasteries were destroyed and the monastics exiled, imprisoned, or executed. In 9th century China, for example, entire schools of Buddhism disappeared after a Tang emperor ordered Buddhism to be eliminated. This threat was a powerful incentive to support political and military leaders who favored them and to cater to the whims of whatever monarch ruled them.

The pattern of religious violence in Europe, while not identical, more often than not also was connected to political power. The wars that broke out after the Reformation, for example, were not over Catholic versus Protestant doctrine but whether Catholic or Protestant monarchs would occupy thrones. The outcomes of those wars determined Catholic and Protestant demographic patterns that persist to this day. Indeed, it seems to me Christianity itself has become the dominant religion only where it has enjoyed some kind of political patronage, beginning with Constantine.

Just as politics supports religion, sometimes religion is put to work for political ends. The infamous Spanish Inquisition was the pet project of the monarchs Ferdinand and Isabella, and not Rome, I understand. Their holinesses Pope Sixtus IV and Pope Innocent VIII appear to have been troubled by it but were not able to stop it without losing the military support of Spain when they feared Rome might be attacked by Turks.

Are the examples above examples of religious violence or political violence? Or religious/political violence? Or political violence joined by religious people? If the labels are important to you, you'd have to look at each situation independently, I think.

It's an inescapable fact that in both Asia and Europe, and probably everywhere else, through most of human civilization religious traditions existed only at the pleasure of rulers, and I cannot emphasize that enough. A religious tradition that fell out of favor with its ruler is one that suffered calamity; see, for example, much of the history of Judaism. Many long-existing religious institutions have made political and even military alliances to survive. I make no value judgments here; that's just how it is.

* * *

It's also the case that people who enter the priesthood, or monastic orders, are still products of their cultures, and their culturally conditioned biases don't evaporate as soon as they shave their heads and put on a robe.

One of the fruits of Buddhist practice is that it enables one to intimately and directly recognize one's cultural conditioning *as* conditioning, so that biases and harmful predilections can be released. Reaching that state doesn't happen overnight, however. For most of us, it takes the sincere effort of at least a few years, even a lifetime.

And in places like Burma, where monks enjoy high status and are somewhat buffered from extreme economic hardship, not everyone who shaves his head and puts on a robe is going to be all that sincere.

Lately I've seen some news stories and commentaries about "Buddhist fundamentalism" in Asia. Others are calling monk-led hate campaigns "Buddhist ethnocentrism." Same thing.

I wrote earlier that a great many factors other than religious belief begat the original Christian fundamentalism. Wherever it exists, religious fundamentalism primarily is a variation of right-wing reactionism. Most of the time, at its core it's an effort to stop some kind of cultural or social change, whether modernity, democracy, loss of racial or sectarian privilege, or in some cases western hegemony. That it's packaged to make it look as if it's just about religion doesn't make it so.

In the case of Buddhist fundamentalism in Asia, as far as I can see scriptural literalism isn't as much of a factor, and there is less obsession with the sexual purity of women than one often sees in fundamentalist movements. Otherwise, though, it pretty much fits the mold. Karen Armstrong wrote,

> It is important to recognize that these theologies and ideologies are rooted in fear. The desire to define doctrines, erect barriers, establish borders, and segregate the faithful in a sacred enclave where the law is stringently observed springs from that terror of extinction which has made all fundamentalists, at one time or another, believe that the secularists were about to wipe them out. [Armstrong, *The Battle for God* (Ballantine, 2000), p. 368]

The violent Burmese Buddhists are bent on making all of Burma a "sacred enclave." Recently some representatives of an international relief agency removed a Buddhist flag that had been placed in front of their headquarters. This was to signal neutrality. But the mobs weren't having it, and the relief agency staff had to be evacuated for their safety.

However irrational, the belief that the Rohingya Muslims represent an existential threat to Burmese Buddhists appears to be a primary factor behind the hate campaign. This is true even though Buddhism explicitly teaches that the self that perceives existential threats is an illusion. The violent Burmese Buddhists clearly are entangled in Buddhism as a tribal identity rather than Buddhism as a spiritual path.

* * *

As is the case with Burma, many of the factors impacting politics and Buddhism in Asia today can be traced back to European colonialism. This is not true of all of it, but it's true of a lot of it. For example, much of the government of China's raging paranoia about foreign religious authority — including the Dalai Lama — can be traced back to the disruptive activities of 19th century European powers and their Christian missionary auxiliaries that culminated in the Boxer Rebellion of 1899-1901.

Like Burma, Sri Lanka has long been dominated by Theravada Buddhism. Sri Lanka also was partly or entirely occupied by European powers for more than four centuries, beginning in 1505, when Portuguese seamen began taking control of the coasts, until 1948, when it achieved independence from Great Britain. A quick review of colonial history in Sri Lanka —formerly called Ceylon — provides some background to developments in Buddhism there today.

Portuguese ships first landed on the shores of Ceylon at a time when the island was home to a number of small and often warring kingdoms. As the Sinhalese (the dominant ethnic group in Sri Lanka) remember it, the Portuguese were particularly brutal toward Buddhists. Parents who refused to have children baptized might see their babes ripped from their arms and tossed to crocodiles. Anyone caught wearing an orange robe was executed on the spot.

Whether this actually happened I do not know, but many Sinhalese *believe* it happened.

Portuguese wantonly destroyed many Buddhist temples and artifacts, the Sinhalese also say. And around 1560 the Portuguese gained possession of the single most sacred thing in Ceylon — a tooth of the Buddha. A king of what is now a portion of Burma offered a handsome reward for the tooth, but the Catholic Archbishop of the region declared the relic must not be ransomed to idolaters, and he smashed the tooth himself. The remnants were burned and tossed into a river. But wait — the king in still-independent Kandy declared that he had the *real* tooth, and the one destroyed by the Archbishop was a fake. So the tooth was saved and is venerated in Sri Lanka to this day.

Make of that what you will.

To get rid of the Portuguese, the king of Kandy invited Holland, which had been warring with Portugal, to come and liberate Ceylon. The result was that the Dutch took control of most of Ceylon in 1658. It is said the remaining Portuguese escaped inland and sought sanctuary from the king of Kandy. Being a devout Buddhist, the king granted it.

The Dutch, who were primarily interested in commerce, were more benevolent toward Buddhism than the Portuguese had been. However, the Sinhalese found there were advantages to converting to Christianity — e.g., higher civil status; better chances of employment. Sinhalese who converted were sometimes called "government Christians."

As part of some convoluted maneuvering during the Napoleonic Wars, Great Britain took Ceylon over from the Dutch in 1796. A few years later British troops marched into Kandy, the last holdout of Sinhalese independence, so Britain was in possession of the entire island. Britain decided that Christianity would have a "civilizing" effect on their colonials and adopted conversion to Christianity as an official policy. Missionaries poured into Ceylon, eager to drag the natives away from their idolatry. Academies opened all over the island to give the young people a proper Christian and English-speaking education. And as with the Dutch, the Sinhalese found that Christian baptism was a prerequisite for employment and business success under British rule

By the mid-19th century, Buddhist institutions in Ceylon were moribund, and Sinhalese laypeople knew very little about Buddhism. But then came the Great Revival.

A charismatic Buddhist monk named Mohottivatte Gunananda (1823-1890) began traveling the island, speaking to rapt and growing audiences and calling for a return to Buddhism. In 1866, Gunananda began a series of public debates with the foremost Christian missionaries in Ceylon. The Buddhist monk had the advantage; he had studied the Christian Bible and also the growing body of rationalist criticism of Christianity being generated in Europe. In Sinhalese eyes the monk triumphed, every time.

In 1880 Gunananda was joined by Henry Steel Olcott (1832-1907), a former New York lawyer and U.S. Civil War veteran who was one of the founders of Theosophy. Among other things, Olcott agitated for Buddhist civil rights and passed out pro-Buddhist, anti-Christian literature. He was a big hit with the Sinhalese, who called him the White Buddhist. Sri Lankan cricket tournaments are named in his honor to this day.[xlvii]

In 1883 Olcott was joined by a young Sinhalese man named David Hewavitharane, who soon ditched his Christian name in favor of Anagarika ("homeless one") Dharmapala ("protector of the dharma"). Anagarika Dharmapala (1864-1933) was from a prominent family and had been well educated in the British Christian academies. He was also handsome, engaging, and brilliant.

Dharmapala and Olcott eventually parted company, mostly because Olcott was never entirely Buddhist. Olcott's religious beliefs were more of a fusion of several Asian traditions mixed in with generous portions of spiritualism and American transcendentalism.

But Dharmapala became thoroughly committed to Buddhism. He soon combined his work to revive Buddhism with calls for national independence, believing that one goal could not be secured without the other. Thus it was that Buddhist revivalism and national independence became one and the same cause for many Sinhalese. Indeed, Dharmapala is credited with creating a Sinhalese national identity that had not existed before, and Buddhism became an essential part of that identity.

Dharmapala's Buddhist revival/national independence campaign had its ups and downs, but by the 1920s many young people were joining up. After Dharmapala's death others stepped into his shoes to carry the Buddhist/nationalist banner, so to speak. Meanwhile, British policies continued to infuriate the people of Ceylon. When the British Raj dissolved in 1947 Britain's hold on Ceylon also became untenable. Ceylon became an independent dominion of the British Commonwealth in 1948 and the Republic of Sri Lanka in 1972.

I say this brief account of Sri Lankan history tells us why Buddhism in Sri Lanka today is so militantly conservative. Centuries of being treated shabbily by their colonial overlords left the Sinhalese with, well, issues. History "has imbued Sinhalese with the sense of being repeatedly under siege," Robert Kaplan wrote. "As a result, like the Serbs in the former Yugoslavia, the Jews in Israel, and the Shiites in Iran, the Sinhalese are a demographic majority with a dangerous minority complex of persecution."[xlviii]

* * *

Today's Sinhalese Buddhists, monk and layperson alike, are hyper-sensitive to disrespect of Buddhism. For example, in 2010 the American vocal artist Akon had his visa revoked and was forced to cancel a sold-out concert in Colombo after he released a video featuring some bikini-clad women dancing in front of a Buddha statue. Also in 2010, a woman who had written two books about her conversion from Buddhism to Islam was arrested for, according to authorities, attempting to send copies of her books through the mail. In 2012 some French tourists photographed themselves kissing a Buddha statue and were arrested and fined for it. In 2013 and 2014, in two separate incidents, British tourists were detained and deported because they had tattoos depicting images of the Buddha.

More seriously, there have been several mob attacks on churches and mosques, and sometimes Buddhist monks have been spotted in the mobs. For example, in 2009 Buddhist monks were videoed throwing stones at a Christian Evangelical church where two women had died, allegedly, after a faith healing. In 2014 seven monks were arrested and charged with vandalizing a couple of churches; why they might have done this I do not know.

In 2012 a Sinhalese monk named Gnanasara organized Bodu Bala Sena, or Buddhist Power Force, which appears to be emulating the anti-Muslim propaganda campaign generated by Wirathu in Burma. Dozens of mosques have been attacked, sometimes during prayer service. The group also calls for boycotts of Muslim-owned businesses and banning the wearing of *hijabs*.

As in Burma, this campaign of violence allegedly is to protect Buddhism. Sri Lanka is 70 percent Buddhist and 10 percent Muslim.

It seems to me that after all the Sinhalese had been through, Buddhism became part of the Sinhalese tribal identity. And as is usually the case with tribal identities, protecting the identity tends to override everything else, including the practice of the Buddha's teaching.

The Sri Lankan Civil War, which raged from 1983 to 2009, involved the island's two largest ethnic groups, the Sinhalese and the Tamils. The Tamils, with their own language and culture, were not newcomers; it's believed they'd inhabited Ceylon for at least a couple of millennia. These two groups had mostly peacefully co-existed for a long time and had even worked together in the national independence movement.

But by the 1970s both the government and the Buddhist establishment of Sri Lanka had adopted the view that Sri Lanka is primarily the land of the Sinhalese people, and the Sinhalese people are somehow ordained to preserve and defend Buddhism from its many enemies. And this view gave the Sinhalese permission, in their minds, to treat Tamils and other non-Sinhalese as second-class citizens.

This happened because the Sinhalese had cultivated both a holy cause and a fanatical grievance. This seems to be the standard recipe for Religions Gone Wrong.

The Tamils are mostly Hindu, although a substantial minority is Christian. This made the new pan-Sinhalese-Buddhist tribal identity something of an issue for them, and for the Sinhalese. Shortly after independence the Tamils felt they were not being treated fairly by the Sinhalese majority, and frankly, often they weren't. Some Tamils began to agitate for fairer treatment and then for a separate Tamil state. Violence escalated, and soon there was a full-scale civil war, and many Tamils and Sinhalese died.

I don't want to take the time here to review all of the issues of the war and the "who-did-what-to-whom" details. For purposes of this discussion, who is to blame for what is less important than how institutional Buddhism in Sri Lanka handled itself regarding the war. And the answer is, not well.

By the early 1980s, monks were taking part in large-scale anti-Tamil demonstrations that sometimes turned violent. As the civil war escalated, the Sinhalese drew upon their founding myths to fortify their rationalizations for their actions. For example, a 5th-century Sinhalese epic poem called the *Mahavamsa* ("great chronicle"), which presents a mythologized quasi-history of early Buddhism in Sri Lanka, was trotted out to provide "historical" precedent for Buddhist violence and a just war theory of sorts. But the *Mahavamsa* is literature, not scripture.

In 2004 monks organized a political party, Jathika Hela Urumaya (JHU), or "National Heritage Party." This was a controversial move that drew criticism from other monks and laypeople as well, but the monks won a few seats in Parliament. JHU advocated wiping out the Tamil guerrillas by force and promoted anti-religious conversion laws aimed mostly at Christian missionaries. Monks also engaged in pro-war demonstrations.

The war ended in 2009 after Tamil civilians were advised to seek safety in a "no fire zone." A UN report from 2012 estimated that about 120,000 civilians were trapped in the NFZ when they were subjected to sustained shelling, allegedly by government forces, although the government continues to deny this. An estimated 40,000 civilians, some of them children, died. At the same time Tamil guerrillas shot civilians trying to escape the NFZ, possibly believing they would be a bargaining chip of sorts.

A few days later, Tamil political leaders were assured they and their families could surrender under a white flag. They presented themselves to the Sri Lanka military, white flags in hand, and (according to many accounts) 18 of them were shot dead. As I write this nearly five years have passed, and Sri Lanka so far has been able to block any significant international investigation into these incidents. Like the government, the Buddhist establishment seems to be pretending none of this ever happened, or if it did happen it was the Tamils' fault.

It must be said that many monks in Sri Lanka stayed out of politics and the war cheerleading. I'm told that sometimes they even drew the wrath of right-wing Buddhists by reaching across ethnic and religious lines. It must also be said that the guerrillas, the Tamil Tigers, were as deadly and ruthless as they come, and several years of being at war with them would mess with anyone's head.

But I've combed through several analyses of the current state of Buddhism in Sri Lanka, and they all (well, all but one) say the same thing — that much of the Buddhist establishment has been corroded by nationalism and notions of the glorious destiny of the Sinhalese people, defenders of the dharma against its enemies. We're back to the messianic thinking called out in the last chapter as the standard fuel for destructive, totalitarian mass movements.

And this takes me to a book titled *Buddhist Warfare*, edited by Michael Jerryson and Mark Juergensmeyer (Oxford University Press, 2010). This book has mightily impressed a lot of people, especially people who know little about either Buddhism or Asian history. Others of us find much of it maddeningly disingenuous.

For example, the chapter on Sri Lanka — "Onward Buddhist Soldiers: Preaching to the Sri Lankan Army" — was written by a then-Ph.D. candidate at the University of Virginia, Daniel Kent, based on Kent's firsthand research in 2004-2007. The chapter provides an interesting and informative snapshot of how Sinhalese Buddhists were struggling to justify and rationalize fighting in battles against the Tamils in light of Buddhist teaching.

However, the chapter says *absolutely nothing* about the centuries of colonialism and the corrupting influence of Sinhalese nationalistic messianism that developed with the independence movement. Kent traveled around Sri Lanka asking questions about karma and other doctrines, and that's fine, but this tells us nothing about the *root* causes of the Buddhist warfare in Sri Lanka, which is what Jerryson and Juergensmeyer claim to be presenting.

* * *

My brief account of Buddhist violence in Sri Lanka and Burma is not intended to make excuses or even blame colonialism. The point is to look at how cultural, social, political, and historical elements come together to push followers of even a non-violent religious tradition into violence.

I have seen way too many commentaries on Sri Lanka and Burma that boil down to, "Oh, snark. Buddhists are violent, too. This proves all religions suck." This isn't helping us understand anything.

I propose that this combination of holy cause/fanatical grievance is at the heart of most group violence, large scale and small. I also propose that any strongly held belief system or ideology could provide the holy cause; it doesn't have to be religion. History shows us that nationalism will do nicely also, especially when combined with belief in a glorious national destiny and the presumed virtues of racial or ethnic purity.

The combination of religious and nationalist fanaticism does seem particularly deadly, however.

* * *

I also propose that we make distinctions between religion as identity and religion as spiritual path. Violent religious factions around the globe appear to share some characteristics, and one of these is a tendency to disregard doctrines that counsel putting away hatred and avoiding violence. In fact, the more radical and violent the group, the less likely the fanatics are to accept their religion's doctrines in any holistic way. Instead, they tend to make a fetish out of some doctrines, usually those involving enforcement of morality and respecting the religion's deities and symbols, while ignoring deeper spiritual doctrines about humility and compassion. We can see this clearly in radical Islam, but the same tendencies are apparent in hyper-conservative Christianity and Judaism as well as in the militant Buddhist monks.

And this tells me there are complexes of social-psychological factors fueling "religious" violence that are not necessarily about religion, or religion as spiritual practice. More often it's about religion as tribal identity, and the violence is about defending the tribe and acting out personal or collective myths.

Americans without graduate degrees in Asian history, which is most of us, generally know next to nothing about Asian history and culture, never mind Buddhism. For this reason, when we hear about Buddhists attacking Tamils or Muslims or some other group, there's a knee-jerk tendency to assume that this is just about Buddhism.

But it's rarely *just* about Buddhism. Or Islam, or Christianity, or Judaism, or any other religion. Like any other part of human civilization, religions exist in a context of culture, society, politics, and history, not to mention the various psychological issues of the participants. Religion *has* been the prime driver of some violent situations, but sometimes it's just one factor among many, and the violence probably would have happened without it.

And sometimes religion may not be the prime driver but acts more as an *accelerant*, or at least an excuse, giving people a moral "cover" or context for their rage, even when their rage is being driven by something else entirely. If you can persuade yourself that your vehemence is sanctified, and that you are entitled or even *anointed* to strike at the object of your anger, it's a lot easier to light the fuse or pull the trigger.

And this, I think, is at the root of why so much of the mass violence in the world today has a connection to religion. Religion has become the last refuge of the furious.

This is why "pro-life" zealots give themselves permission to assassinate doctors. This explains how some of the September 11 terrorists, according to many reports, were heavy drinkers and "night clubbers," in violation of Islamic law. This is how a Burmese Buddhist monk can spread hate speech about a despised minority group, in spite of the clear teaching of the Metta Sutta, which he surely has been chanting for years:

> Let none deceive another, or despise any being in any state. Let none through anger or ill-will wish harm upon another. Even as a mother protects with her life her child, her only child, so with a boundless heart should one cherish all living beings; radiating kindness over the entire world; spreading upwards to the skies, and downwards to the depths; outwards and unbounded, freed from hatred and ill-will. [from the Metta Sutta, translated from the Pali Tipitika by the Amaravati Sangha]

Because, deep down, what they're doing *is not really about religion.*

By that I mean religion is not the prime motivator; fear, hate, greed, and ignorance are the prime motivators. Religion is just the permission slip. And this is particularly remarkable when you consider that many of the teachings of the long-established religious traditions are intended to mitigate fear, hate and greed, and sometimes even ignorance.

It's also why discussions, including academic studies, of religious violence that don't look at the entire context, that try to explain religious violence by considering *only* doctrine, are a waste of time.

* * *

There is no justification for violence in the canonical Mahayana sutras with which I am familiar. However, in an essay in the aforementioned *Buddhist Warfare* book Stephen Jenkins, chair of religious studies at Humboldt State University, analyzes a sutra allegedly condoning violence. It is called the Ārya-Bodhisattva-gocara-upāyaisaya-vikurvāna-nirdeśa-nāma-mahāyāna-sūtra, and I regret there are several diacritical marks left out of that title because they aren't in my font set. The short form of the title is Ārya-Satyakaparivarta, but why cut corners?

What follows may go further into Buddhist doctrinal minutia than might be interesting to many of you, and I apologize for that, but there's a purpose for it.

The essay has the alarming title "Making Merit Through Warfare and Torture According to the Ārya-Bodhisattva-gocara-upāyaisaya-vikurvāna-nirdeśa-Sutra," dropping the "nāma-mahāyāna" part of the su-tra's name. Making merit is something one hears about a lot in Buddhism. Spiritual practice and doing good deeds for others accumulate "merit" that contributes toward enlightenment. Note that on several levels this makes no literal sense to me; I'm just explaining what it is.

There is only one published English translation of this sutra that I could find, by Lozang Jamspal (*The Range of the Bodhisattva, a Mahayana Sutra*, American Institute of Buddhist Studies, 2010), which Professor Jenkins cites as the translation he is using. So I acquired a copy and read it.

And I couldn't find any part of the sutra that said Buddhists can make merit through warfare and torture.

Truly puzzled, I went back to Jenkins's essay and read it again, more carefully. I realized then that he was not analyzing the scripture itself as much pointing to its textual similarities to other scriptures, both Buddhist and Hindu. His argument is that several *other* Buddhist and Hindu texts that use similar wording — especially if you skip the Chinese translation and compare the Tibetan to the Sanskrit, although the hypothetical Sanskrit original was lost centuries ago, according to Lozang Jamspal, so any Sanskrit version we have today probably was translated from a Chinese translation — and these other texts appear to be claiming that torture and warfare will make merit, according to a couple of other western religious studies scholars Jenkins cites, so this is what this sutra says, also, even though it doesn't say that. And I am not making this up; that's the argument.

I can't speak for the Hindu texts, but Jenkins's arguments *vis à vis* other Buddhist scriptures are, um, flimsy.

For example, one of the other texts cited as condoning violence is a sutta (that's Pali for *sutra*) in the Pali Sutta-pitaka called the Cula-Saccaka Sutta[xlix], which is the 35th text in a section called the Majjhima Nikaya, or Middle-Length Discourses, if you want to look it up. There are translations online if you want to read it yourself.

The Pali sutta describes a debate between the Buddha and a character named Saccaka, who is addressed as Aggivessana, which is a reference to his family. My reading of the sutta does not match Jenkins's description of it, however. For example, Jenkins says that the Buddha was accompanied by a "menacing armed bodyguard" named Vajrapani who threatened Saccaka's life. I have two translations at hand, one by Bhikkhu Nanamoli and Bhikkhu Bodhi (the translation Jenkins cites)[1] and another by Thanissaro Bhikkhu, which is online at Access to Insight. Both translations describe Vajrapani as a spirit who appears in the air, unbidden, and (as I will explain in a bit) it seems to me the "threat" as well as the spirit are metaphorical. I understand the 5th century Theravadin scholar Buddhaghosa identified Vajrapani as Indra, the Hindu king of *devas* who appears as a benevolent character in some early Buddhist texts. Where Jenkins gets "bodyguard" I have no idea.

But I'm getting ahead of things. Jenkins writes,

> The key question put to Saccaka by Sakyamuni Buddha shows a connection to the later Mahayana Sutra. The question is whether an anointed king may exercise the power in his own realm to execute those who should be executed. The Buddha's argument hinges on the fact that this is so.

Stop there. The key question of the sutta, stated several times, is whether the *skandhas* are the self. Very briefly, the skandhas are the five aggregates of components that make up a person — form (the body), sensation, perception/cognition, discrimination/predilections, and awareness. The Buddha taught that the skandhas are not the self — this is a very basic teaching that he repeated several times — and Saccaka was going around saying that they are *too* the self. The Buddha's argument isn't *about* kings and executions; as we will see, he was just using kings and executions as a debating device to lure Saccaka into a trap, a point that eludes Professor Jenkins.

Jenkins continues,

> Saccaka concedes that an anointed king could indeed exercise the power of capital punishment and he would be worthy (Pali: *arahati*) to exercise it. He strengthens the point by saying that this would be true even for groups and societies that do not have such kings. So the Buddha forces Saccaka, under threat of death, to concede that an anointed king both has and merits the power to execute criminals.

This makes no sense. Saccaka had already said kings could execute criminals, and if you read the sutta, you see the threat hadn't been issued yet when Saccaka said that, so why did the Buddha have to threaten him to concede something he had already said? And the answer is, *the actual text of the sutta says something else entirely*.

After Saccaka issued his opinion on kings and executions — which was completely un-coerced — the Buddha's next question was, "What do you think, Aggivessana? When you say, 'Form is my self,' do you wield power over that form: 'May my form be thus, may my form not be thus'?"

The Buddha's point is that the skandhas are *not* the self because they are not subject to the mastery of the self. What cannot be brought under one's complete mastery or control cannot be identified as "my self."

And at this point Saccaka realized he had just lost the debate, so he refused to answer the question, and when he refused to answer a second time the spirit Vajrapani appeared, carrying an "iron thunderbolt," or *vajra*, in this usage a weapon/ritual object also associated with Indra. The spirit threatened to split Saccaka's head into seven pieces if he didn't answer the question. The terrified Saccaka looked to the Buddha for refuge and thereby accepted his teaching on the nature of the self. And I could easily write another 20,000 words on why Saccaka's terror was not for his physical life but was more about the challenge to his self-identity; an existential threat of sorts, yes, *but not to his body*.

Professor Jenkins interprets Vajrapani's threat as a literal death threat. I believe he is misunderstanding idioms. In English we sometimes use violent idioms to describe non-violent competition. Someone may be "crushed" or "get his ass kicked" in a debate, for example. This doesn't mean the individual was physically crushed or kicked.

Likewise, splitting heads into various numbers of pieces comes up occasionally in old Buddhist texts, and in context it usually refers to some kind of mental breakdown, not death. For example, in the Candima Sutta of the Pali Tipitika, a character named Rahu had seized another character named Candima but was compelled to let her go, saying, "If I had not released Candima my head would have split into seven pieces. **While yet I live, I should have had no happiness.**"[lii] (Emphasis added.)

Bottom line, the question being put to Saccaka that he refused to answer had nothing to do with kings and executions but was instead about the nature of the self. And there's nothing in the text that suggests the Buddha thinks executions are *praiseworthy*. The question was merely a debating device drawing on the fact that kings in that culture pretty much had absolute authority in the matter of sentencing criminals. And if this sutta is supposed to be a basis for the Ārya-Bodhisattva-gocara-upāyaisaya-vikurvāna-nirdeśa-nāma-mahāyāna-sūtra, it must be pointed out that the later sutra explicitly advises *against* capital punishment. So even if the Cula-Saccaka Sutta said what Jenkins thinks it said, that supposed connection still doesn't make sense.

So what *does* the Ārya-Bodhisattva-gocara-upāyaisaya-vikurvāna-nirdeśa-nāma-mahāyāna-sūtra say about warfare and torture?

Regarding torture, the speaker in the sutra, a sage named Satyavadin, advises that a king should chastise people in a benevolent manner, which is explained this way --

> When a ruler believes that punishment [of the wicked] will not be effected by means of mere obloquy, then, concentrating on love and compassion and without resort to killing, damaging of sense organs, or cutting off of limbs, he should try warning, scolding, rebuking, or beating them, or confiscating their property, exiling them from the state, tying them up, or imprisoning them. A ruler should be tough, but not in any heavier ways than these.

Variations of this same wording are repeated several times and constitute the sutra's advice for handling unrepentant prisoners. Here in the 21st century we do think of tying people up and beating them as "torture," but I'm not sure the people who lived when this sutra was written (15 to 20 centuries ago, give or take) would have seen it that way. Beating may have seemed benevolent in comparison to other available options of the time, particularly if the sense organs were not to be damaged. But that's as close to advocating "torture" as the sutra gets. And then *if* the chastised individual mends his ways and behaves responsibly, the king obtains merit. And he would obtain the same merit if he could get the prisoner to reform by reading him poetry. The punishment itself is not what earns the merit.

As far as warfare is concerned, the sutra explicitly denies any merit to wars of conquest or aggression. A ruler may use arms to defend his kingdom and protect his people, but he may only use as much force as is necessary to expel invaders, and then he must not seek to punish the invaders but instead try to make peace with them. Even better, he should do what he can to prevent war in the first place, such as settling disputes or making alliances with other kingdoms so that an aggressive foreign king would think twice about starting a war.

If invasion is unavoidable, the king is advised to deploy his forces in an advantageous manner to ensure victory. Injuring and killing the invaders should be avoided if possible, although it is acknowledged that this may not be possible. But if the king has sincerely done his best to avoid war, if the self-defense is carried out so that there is no punishment or vengeance heaped upon the invaders, and if the king "undertakes these measures for the protection of the people and for the sake of their families, wives, and children without concern for himself and his property and possessions, he greatly will increase his immeasurable merit."

So there's your "making merit through warfare." Let's just say the essay's title, as well as many claims made in Jenkins's essay, are a tad misleading. Oxford University Press needs to answer for publishing this.

I hope this isn't boring the stuffing out of you, but I think it's important to call these things out, because western religious studies scholars sometimes make points about Buddhism based on garbled readings of texts or misunderstandings of doctrines, and this stuff gets published in academic journals and cited by other western religious studies scholars and taught in classes. And there is something of a trend in western Buddhist studies in which, in the name of "objectivity," Buddhist texts are being mis-interpreted to be about violence. This isn't the only example.

Bottom line, I still know of no Buddhist scripture, Theravada or Mahayana, that condones violence. This is not to say that Buddhists have never rationalized or made excuses for violence; of course they have. And sometimes they cite Buddhism in their rationalizations, but they cannot *honestly* base those rationalizations on doctrine or scripture.

* * *

We've seen that violence in Burma and Sri Lanka appear to be linked to a kind of messianic thinking, or Buddhist millenarianism, that crept into everyone's heads from *somewhere*. There have been messianic movements in Mahayana history also, some of which have been violent. But *Buddhism is not a messianic religion*. So where is this coming from?

Back in Chapter 7, on true believers and mass movements, I speculated that messianic religion is not *necessarily* responsible for messianic politics, but rather that both spring from some deep place in the human psyche. This is just a hypothesis, of course. But Buddhism seems to give us an example of messianic thinking that is *not* supported by religious doctrine, but which keeps creeping into both religion and politics, anyway.

Some of these Buddhist millennial cults have centered on an iconic figure from Mahayana Buddhism named Maitreya, or "a person of loving kindness." I wrote earlier that the dharma — the Buddha's teaching, in this usage — is said to have been forgotten and re-discovered in an endless cycle of time. The Pali scriptures tell us that when "our" Buddha's teaching is entirely forgotten, a person of loving kindness — Maitreya — will re-discover it and teach it just as our historical Buddha did, 25 or so centuries ago. Here is the relevant passage translated from the Cakkavatti Sutta of the Pali Sutta-pitaka (Digha Nikaya 26), describing what will happen the next time the dharma is forgotten:

> Fierce hatred will arise, fierce malevolence, fierce rage, and murderous thoughts: mother for child, child for mother, father for child, child for father, brother for sister, sister for brother. Ultimately, conditions will deteriorate to the point of a "sword-interval," in which swords appear in the hands of all human beings, and they hunt one another like game. A few people, however, will take shelter in the wilderness to escape the carnage, and when the slaughter is over, they will come out of hiding and resolve to take up a life of skillful and virtuous action again. With the recovery of virtue, the human life span will gradually increase again until it reaches 80,000 years, with people attaining sexual maturity at 500. Only three diseases will be known at that time: desire, lack of food, and old age. Another Buddha — Metteyya [*Maitreya* in Pali] — will gain Awakening, his monastic Sangha numbering in the thousands. The greatest king of the time, Sankha, will go forth into homelessness and attain arahantship under Metteyya's guidance. [Thanissaro Bhikkhu translation [liii]]

And that's all the Theravada canonical scriptures say about Maitreya. In fact, I understand some scholars suspect even that much was written in later.

Mahayana Buddhism makes a much bigger deal out of Maitreya. The myth of the Mahayana Maitreya, which may have been partly based on an Indo-Iranian deity, says that Maitreya is the future Buddha who exists now as a *bodhisattva*, or enlightenment being, abiding in the Tusita Heaven, which is one of the 31 realms I mentioned in an earlier chapter. Early depictions of him often show him either standing or sitting in a chair with his feet on the ground, rather than cross-legged, so that he is always ready to stand and go where he is needed.

The chubby, laughing Buddha so often depicted in Chinese art is a beloved character from folklore named Budai (or Pu-tai), who is something like the Chinese Santa Claus, bestowing blessings wherever he goes. He carries a bag full of good things for children and is known to be a protector of the poor and helpless. Budai was absorbed into Chinese Mahayana Buddhism, where he is considered to be an emanation or rebirth of Maitreya. The giant Leshan Buddha of China is a Maitreya, carved in the 8th century to protect travelers on a particularly dangerous stretch of river. In short, Maitreya is a benevolent figure who already *is* to many Mahayana Buddhists.

Beginning in the 4th and 5th centuries, however, China saw recurring outbreaks of violent apocalyptic cults, and these often were organized around the iconic figure of Maitreya. The most notorious of these cult leaders was Faqing, a one-time Buddhist monk who in 550 proclaimed himself to be Maitreya, raised an army, and attacked monasteries that didn't recognize him as their lord. When Faqing's cult soldiers captured a monastery or convent, they slaughtered the monks or nuns as "demons" and destroyed the icons in it. And if a soldier killed ten "demons," he was promoted to the rank of "Tenth-Stage Bodhisattva."

The story of Faqing is widely cited as "Buddhist violence," but I say the story of Faqing has "charismatic psychopath" written all over it. He sounds like a Chinese equivalent of Jim Jones, and like Jones, he had gone so far off the doctrinal reservation that nothing he did could justifiably be attributed to his earlier religious affiliation. Indeed, Faqing could just as easily have called himself Jesus and used Christianity for the same purpose, had anyone in 6th century China heard of it.

I suppose it's a bit late to call in Faqing and his followers for psych evaluations, but I say that whatever was going on with them, the Buddha's teaching wasn't to blame for it. The only recognizably "Buddhist" thing about Faqing and his cult was the icon Maitreya, taken out of context. This illustrates that familiar religious icons and symbols may also have cultural power that can be severed from religious doctrine and used for non-religious purposes.

I understand waves of violent Maitreya cults also recurred in Thailand in the 18th through 20th centuries. This seems odd, since Thai Buddhism is Theravadin, and in Theravada Buddhism Maitreya usually is more of a footnote than an icon. I propose that these cults were examples of messianic thinking emerging from a collective subconscious and co-opting a religious/cultural symbol rather than religious teaching causing the messianic thinking.

Maitreya also has been adopted by non-Buddhists, including the 19th century Theosophists, as some sort of coming world teacher who will save us from our follies. There are a number of websites naming Maitreya as the Antichrist; views differ as to whether this is a good or bad thing. I understand the late L. Ron Hubbard claimed to be Maitreya, or at least dropped broad hints to that effect.

More recently a dotty but probably harmless fellow named Benjamin Crème told readers of the *Guardian* (UK) that Maitreya has arrived and had appeared to millions on American television.[liii] Alas, I missed him, unless Maitreya was that guy on several channels selling kitchen gadgets. He seemed nice.

*   *   *

Now I will bite the bullet, so to speak, and address violence in Japanese Zen.

Brief history: Buddhism was introduced to Japan in the 6th century by a delegation from Korea. Over the centuries several schools of Mahayana Buddhism were imported from mainland Asia, mostly from China. Zen — called Chan in China — was among the last of these, reaching Japan initially at the end of the 12th century. Zen grew in prominence and influence during the Muromachi Period (1336–1573), when it made a huge impact on Japanese art and culture and enjoyed the patronage of the nobility.

The warlord Oda Nobunaga overthrew the government of Japan in 1573, which began what's called the Momoyama Period (1573-1603). Nobunaga and his successor, Toyotomi Hideyoshi, attacked and destroyed one Buddhist monastery after another until institutional Buddhism in Japan was under the warlords' control.

Buddhism survived, and many of the temples and monasteries were rebuilt by the shogunate during the Edo Period (1603–1867), but overall the influence of Buddhism, Zen included, in Japan has been in a state of slow decline ever since. It was replaced by Shinto as the national religion of Japan in the 19th century.

One of the things "everybody knows" about Japanese history is that the famous samurai were much influenced by Zen, which is supposed to be proof that Zen Buddhism has a violent streak. It's true that there is a Zen-Samurai connection. However, after wading through several sources, I've come to believe that connection has been hyped and romanticized out of proportion to what it actually was, especially by authors of popular books about Zen.

Some of this can be traced to one of the first books about Zen published in English. In 1913 a Japanese Soto Zen priest and university professor who was lecturing at Harvard wrote and published *Religion of the Samurai: A Study of Zen Philosophy and Discipline in China and Japan*. Among other inaccurate claims, the author, Nukariya Kaiten (1867-1934) wrote that "As regards Japan, it [Zen] was first introduced into the island as the faith first for the Samurai or the military class, and moulded the characters of many distinguished soldiers whose lives adorn the pages of her history."

I believe Heinrich Dumoulin's *Zen Buddhism: A History, Volume 2: Japan* (Macmillan, 1990), although not without flaw, is as detailed a history of the introduction of Zen to Japan as there is in English, and Dumoulin doesn't mention samurai at all during the "introductory phase." So what actually happened?

What actually happened is that nearly a century after Rinzai Zen (one of the two primary schools of Japanese Zen) was introduced to Japan, samurai took an interest in it and began practicing with Rinzai masters. Rinzai sometimes has a Marine boot camp feel to it, so I can see the appeal. The intensive concentration of Rinzai-style meditation also can be an aid in enhancing martial arts skills and reducing fear of death on a battlefield. The patronage of samurai brought many perks to Rinzai, so many masters were happy to cater to it.

One lineage[liv] of Rinzai Zen in Japan, called O-to-kan, kept itself apart from the politics and patronage of Kyoto and other urban centers, however, and did not particularly cater to samurai. Ironically, this is the only surviving Rinzai lineage in Japan today. The samurai-catering lineages faded away some centuries back. The other major school of Japanese Zen, Soto, never was notably popular with samurai.

So what Nukariya Kaiten wrote was not historically accurate. It seems to me he was both promoting Zen to unknowing westerners and also reflecting growing militaristic romanticism common to his generation in Japan. In other words, he was making a case that was more romance and marketing than history, but it was a case that was uncritically repeated by authors of many popular Zen books that followed.

Yes, Zen influenced Muromachi and Momoyama Period samurai, as it did most of Japanese culture and society at that time. And yes, there is a connection between Zen and Japanese martial arts. Zen originated in China's Shaolin monastery, so Zen and martial arts have long been associated. There is also a connection between Zen and Japanese flower arranging, calligraphy, poetry (notably haiku), bamboo flute playing and the tea ceremony. The esthetics of Zen thoroughly saturated Japanese culture for a long time, especially during the 14th through 16th centuries.

Going back to Zen's formative years in China as Chan Buddhism, the practice has been said to have five "levels" or types of Zen, the names of which I only know in Japanese. The first two, *bonpu* ("unenlightened person") and *gedo* ("outside way") are Zen without Buddhism; the practice of Zen meditation and mindfulness without the context of doctrine. An example of bonpu Zen would be someone using Zen meditation to reduce stress. Father Thomas Merton's practice of Zen meditation to have a Christian mystical experience is an example of gedo Zen — using Zen practices in the context of another religious tradition. The classic example of gedo is practicing Zen to develop supernatural powers, although I don't know that's ever worked for anyone. Someone using Zen meditation to increase mental focus and enhance martial arts skills would be somewhere between bonpu and gedo Zen, I think, and it's my understanding that's what most of the samurai Zen students were doing. But Buddhist teaching is absent from those levels.

So, unlike the Shaolin monks of China who (until recently) were Buddhist monks first and warriors second, it's probably more accurate to say that the samurai were warriors who, for a time, adapted Zen practices but were not necessarily *religious* about it. I understand some samurai pursued Zen at the higher levels, but many did not.

After the Momoyama period ended in 1603 and peace was restored, the samurai warrior culture slowly faded, and the once-fierce samurai evolved into bureaucrats.

* * *

The other matter that must be addressed is the connection between Zen and Japanese militarism in the 20th century, especially during the 1930s and 1940s.

When Brian Daizen Victoria's book *Zen at War* was first published in 1997, I remember sitting in the zendo at Zen Mountain Monastery, listening to the abbot, Daido Roshi, tell us that we must accept the truth whether we like it or not. Victoria's book describes the way the Japanese Zen establishment supported and even encouraged the militarism and military conquests of the early 20th century that culminated in the War in the Pacific. Some of the venerable Zen masters called out for war mongering included teachers in his own lineage, which for Daido Roshi must have been like finding out your beloved grandfather was a serial killer.

Still, Daido endorsed the book and told us it was important to not look away, but to study and learn from the mistakes of others. From what I could see, this was the attitude of most Zen teachers in North America at the time. Some prominent Zen teachers in Japan also issued apologies, sometimes on behalf of their own deceased teachers.

There's no question that the Zen establishment thoroughly prostituted itself to support Japanese militarism in the early 20th century. However, I should also point out that the book *Zen at War* is not above criticism. For example, an essay by Daisetsu Teitaro (D.T.) Suzuki (1870-1966) that allegedly influenced Japanese militarism in the 1930s was first published in the 1950s, according to other scholars. [lv] Suzuki wrote a lot of popular English-language books about Zen, some of which hyped the Zen-samurai connection, so I can't excuse him entirely.

Robert Aitken Roshi also criticized the book, saying, "Unlike the other researchers, Victoria writes in a vacuum. He extracts the words and deeds of Japanese Buddhist leaders from their cultural and temporal context, and judges them from a present-day, progressive, Western point of view."

It should be noted that Aitken Roshi was an American civilian in Japanese-occupied Guam when Japan bombed Pearl Harbor. He was taken into custody shortly after the bombing and spent the entire Pacific war in civilian prisons in Japan. His cell mate, R. H. Blyth, was a student of Zen who had been teaching English in Japan when the war began, and it was Blyth who introduced Aitken to Zen. After the war Aitken became a student of Yasutani Hakuun Roshi, who had been one of the more egregious war-pushers. So he was possibly not all that objective, but he was also closer to what actually happened than most other westerners.

So what did happen?

A little more historical background: During the Meiji Era (1868–1912) Japan rapidly and radically retooled itself into a modern nation. The realization that those stupid, uncouth westerners had gotten ahead of them in technology and science hit the Japanese hard, I understand.

Buddhism initially was banned by the Meiji Emperor in 1868 and was replaced by emperor-worshiping Shinto as the national religion. Many monasteries were closed and large numbers of nuns and monks were forced to return to lay life. In time the Emperor relented and allowed Buddhist institutions to continue, but he imposed conditions that included an end to celibacy.

The change from celibate monks to married priests might not seem like a bad thing, but in Japan it had the effect of turning temples into family businesses. Smaller temples in Japan today often are little more than a priest and his sons making a living by offering funeral and memorial services. But this is taking us away from the subject a bit.

By the end of the 19th century the Japanese appeared to be a people obsessed with affirming who they were. In a period equal to a single human life span Japan had gone from being an isolated, deeply traditional and highly structured neo-Confucian society to being a modern world power. In the process, many generations-old social structures had been replaced abruptly by new ones. It seems that to "find" themselves during this time, the Japanese reached deeply into a romanticized, mythic past while confirming their status as a mighty, and modern, nation through military power. At the same time Buddhism, including Zen, was struggling to find its footing with the government and within the new realities of monastic life. That's no excuse for what happened next, but it may tell us something about where peoples' heads were at the time.

Brian Victoria wrote in *Zen at War* that Buddhism's displacement by Shinto shook Buddhist institutions to the core, and they responded with a "New Buddhism" meant to prove that Buddhists could be patriotic and subservient to the Emperor, too. This was one of the factors that sent many Japanese Buddhist institutions, not just Zen, down a pro-war rabbit hole. Doctrines of compassion and nonviolence were shamelessly twisted to support militarism and the conquest of other Asian nations.

Uchiyama Gudo (1874-1911), a Soto Zen priest who spoke out against the corruption of doctrine in service to militarism, was accused of plotting to assassinate the Emperor and executed. Zen authorities were compelled to apologize publicly for his behavior. From then on, in Japan "through the end of the Pacific War no major Buddhist or Christian leader ever again spoke out in any organized way against government policies, either civilian or military, domestic or foreign," Victoria writes.

Indeed, from then until the end of World War II Zen institutions supported whatever the Japanese military did, atrocities and all, and issued declarations about killing in warfare being the "manifestation of highest wisdom."

This is stunningly shocking, especially for those of us who know what Zen teachings actually teach. Was this betrayal of dharma the result of cowardice? Or were these priests and teachers genuinely sucked into the same groupthink that had infested the rest of Japan? Someone who has more knowledge of the place and period than I do will have to answer that. Either way, there's no excuse for this. It was a colossal failure on the part of Japanese Zen.

* * *

When is religious violence not really religious violence? Put another way, is there a significant difference between violence caused by religion versus violence caused by historical, sociological, nationalistic, or even psychological factors that have possessed and overwritten religion?

When you are talking about "religious violence" or a particular religion being violent, it's important to clarify what you mean. Are you talking about the original teachings of the revered founder? Are you talking about the institutions that came after? Are you talking about folk beliefs that cultures mix into their religions but which have nothing to do with what the revered founder taught (the Easter Bunny, for example, not that the Easter Bunny is violent)? Are you talking about the actions of everyone who self-identifies as followers of that religion, however superficially? Are you talking about some rogue psychopath who used some bastardized version of the teachings to manipulate his followers?

Here are my criteria:

Violence is "religious" when it is advocated or condoned by canonical scripture or orthodox doctrine.

Violence is "religious" when it is advocated or condoned by established religious institutions.

Violence is "religious" when it is initiated by clergy or laypeople for the purpose of promoting or defending that religion.

As far as Buddhism goes, I still do not know of any canonical scripture or orthodox doctrine that condones violence, but certainly there are many examples in Buddhist history of the other two types of religious violence.

However, not every episode labeled "religious violence" meets these criteria.

Back in the 1930s a Japanese cult headed by a man named Nisshō Inoue carried out political assassinations. Inoue called himself a priest of Nichiren Buddhism, but he was never ordained, and I'm reasonably certain no sect of Nichiren Buddhism claimed him as its own. He was a fake, in other words. Yet Nisshō Inoue and his band of cutthroats are frequently presented as examples of "Buddhist violence."

Let's expand this a bit. Inoue apparently was "inspired" by the Lotus Sutra, which he believed supported his extremist right-wing, hypernationalistic views. However, I have read two translations of the Lotus Sutra, and I say Inoue was in tap-dancing toasted cheese sandwich territory. He was reading something into the scripture that isn't there.

Are we talking about "Buddhist violence" or "whackjob violence"?

Back in 1995 members of a cult called Aum Shinrikyo released sarin gas in a Tokyo subway, killing several people. The founder of Aum Shinkrikyo, Shoko Asahara, declared in one of his books that he is Jesus, and his doctrines were mostly inspired by the book of Revelations in the New Testament, with elements from popular culture, yoga, and Shinto and Buddhist iconography mixed in. Asahara was not ordained and had no affiliation with any religious institution, Buddhist or otherwise.

Yet, somehow, the sarin gas attacks keep turning up on lists of "Buddhist violence." I believe this is largely because Michael Jerryson wrote in the introduction to *Buddhist Warfare* —

Buddhist messianic violence persists in contemporary times, with the latest violent outbreak occurring in Japan. In 1995, Asahara Shoko's Aum Shinrikyo unleashed Sarin nerve gas into the Tokyo subway, killing a dozen people and injuring many more. Part of Aum Shinrikyo's ideologies is based on the *Lotus Sutra*, one of the most popular and influential *sutras* (scriptures) in Mahayana Buddhism.

This is profoundly dishonest. It clearly implicates the Lotus Sutra as the inspiration for the sarin gas attack. *But there is nothing in the Lotus Sutra that advocates violence against anyone.* Just the opposite, actually.

I've looked for a connection between Aum Shinrikyo and the Lotus Sutra, and all I've found so far is that Asahara mentioned it in an interview. But the Lotus Sutra is somewhat totemic in Japanese culture, something like the way the Ten Commandments are totemic to right-wing Christians who can only remember half of them but believe in their power, anyway. Asahara might have invoked the name of the sutra just to give himself more religious authority. This doesn't mean he ever read it.

And sometimes people are psychotic. You might remember the sad story of Andrea Yates, a Texas woman who in 2001 drowned her five children in a bathtub. Initial stories made much of the Yates family's association with a conservative Christian congregation. I saw a lot of knee-jerk blaming of religion for the children's deaths.

But it turns out Yates was massively psychotic, had been for some time, and had just had her anti-psychotic meds abruptly discontinued by an apparently incompetent doctor less than a week before she killed her children. Even the consulting psychiatrists of the Harris County Jail voluntarily came forward to testify at her first trial that Yates's mental state was as far gone as mental states can go. She had to be fed a cocktail of anti-psychotic meds every day so that she could quietly sit in a chair through the trail, although whether she had any idea what was going on is questionable. After a second trial she was found not guilty by reason of insanity and is still hospitalized as of this writing.

I'm no psychiatrist, but I suspect psychiatric disorders of *that* severity aren't caused by religious beliefs, but by some kind of brain impairment.

Psychopathic cult leaders are still with us, also. My understanding is that all sorts of perfectly normal people get sucked into cults. As discussed in Chapter 7, followers of any authoritarian mass movement give up some of their autonomy and submerge their individual identities with that of the group. In extreme cases, the followers can be thoroughly brainwashed. But such movements are not necessarily religious, and when they are religious they are nearly always more about emotional dependence on the leader and the group than devotion to gods or doctrines. Religion is just the packaging.

In fact, it seems to me that one of the common indicators of a genuinely dangerous, manipulative cult leader is a tendency to make doctrines up as he goes along, to suit his moods. If he originally had some association with an established religion, that association will have been severed, and whatever he teaches will become increasingly heterodox and self-serving. Watch out for that.

* * *

What I hope to have illustrated is that religious violence is a complex issue that isn't just about religion. However, when religion is mixed into an already hostile situation it can have an accelerant effect, making violence more likely. Violence is especially likely where religious identity is strongly connected to national or ethnic identity.

If you step far enough back into history, you *can* find people coming to blows over doctrine. For example, in his book *When Jesus Became God: The Struggle to Define Christianity during the Last Days of Rome* (Harcourt, 1999), Richard Rubenstein describes early Christians fighting in the streets over the doctrine of Trinity and proposes that the "heretic" Arius

(d. 336) may have been poisoned by Saint Athanasius (d. 373) to settle the matter.

But most of the time, when you look at any particular episode of religious violence in all of its contexts, actual religious doctrine has little to do with it. When religious institutions engage in violence, the motive is nearly always connected to politics, establishing or protecting institutional authority, or resisting social change. When individuals engage in religious violence, most of the time, religious *identity* is a more critical factor than religious doctrine or devotion, because a challenge to identity can *feel* like a threat to the self. People might *argue* about doctrine, but they'll kill — flushing anti-violence doctrine down the toilet, if need be — to protect the self.

And then if you merge religious identity with national or racial identity, make the protection and defense of that identity a holy cause, and toss in a fanatical grievance about *something* — well, keep your head down, and try to stay out of the cross fire.

9 The Wisdom of Doubt

> Every religion is true one way or another. It is true when understood metaphorically. But when it gets stuck in its own metaphors, interpreting them as facts, then you are in trouble. — Joseph Campbell

Let me tell you an ancient myth I just made up.

Once upon a time the great and all-powerful goddess Betty decided the void was boring, so she made the cosmos. And to make things even more interesting, on one of the prettier side-planets she made life. She may have made life on other planets, also, but somebody else is going to have to make up those myths.

Anyway, pretty soon (in goddess years) this resulted in the formation of a couple of human beings — let's call them Adam and Eve — who enjoyed their lives very much.

There was One Forbidden Thing, as there so often is in ancient myths, which was to eat the fruit of the tree of knowledge of good and evil. But one day a snake told them to go ahead and eat the fruit. *The only reason Betty doesn't want you to eat the fruit is that it will make you as smart as she is, and she doesn't want the competition*, the snake said. *Trust me.*

But when they ate the fruit (characters in these stories always do the One Forbidden Thing; otherwise there wouldn't be a story) they didn't feel wise and powerful. Instead, they recognized their nakedness and separateness, their vulnerability and limitations, and for the first time they knew shame and worry.

Then Betty appeared and said, "You blew it, people. You did the One Forbidden Thing. From now on, humans will feel severed from the rest of Creation. Women will have pain in childbirth because their babies will have grapefruit-size heads to hold baby human brains. You will have to work for a living. And your descendants will need psychiatrists and lawyers. Way to go."

This is, of course, a loose interpretation of the biblical Garden of Eden myth. There's a lot in that myth that underscores a paternalistic worldview, and of course I don't much care for those parts. But the fruit-eating bit is fascinating. What does it say about knowledge of good and evil? What does it say about human consciousness and judgments of right and wrong? There's lots of juicy stuff to contemplate in that story. I dare say you can find a lot of truth in there, if you look for it.

And the terrible irony is that those who insist the story itself is factual, not myth, squeeze all the truth out of it.

The language of *mythos* often is contrasted with the language of *logos*. *Mythos* and *logos* are both Greek words that refer to speaking. Over the centuries philosophers and theologians have used these words to mean several different things, but *logos* generally refers to reason, or to facts and principles that can be objectively observed and verified. *Mythos* refers to a narrative that cannot be verified but may be understood intuitively.

I've observed that some people don't "get" mythos. This is unrelated to general intelligence, as I've observed this phenomenon in both the bright and the dull. And if you don't "get" mythos, I'm not sure you can be taught to get it. I postulate that being mythos-challenged may be something like being tone deaf or color blind; some wires are miswired, somewhere, and thought processes remain rigidly stuck in linear logical mode. Linear logical mode is grand for some sorts of things, but I feel sorry for anyone who can't understand the world in any other way. To me, that would be like going through life with blinkers you can't remove, or with roller skates glued to your feet — sometimes useful, but often a handicap.

The mythos-challenged often object to myths and metaphors because they aren't true, by which they mean they are not *factual*. Of course, the Garden of Eden story is not factual. Adam and Eve and the rest of the characters in the story, including God, are archetypes, not historical figures. The Garden is not a "real" geographic place. The story doesn't tell us anything about biology on this planet or how our species came to be.

However, if we take a cue from Carl Jung and place the Garden in the human psyche, the story resonates with a different kind of truth. Jung understood myths to be ways that the unconscious revealed itself to the conscious mind, and I think there's something to that. At the very least, the great myths that have endured through the centuries illuminate *something* about how humans throughout time have experienced their lives and themselves, for those so inclined to contemplate them.

I've always found it fascinating that it was *knowledge* of good and evil that put an end to paradise, not evil-doing itself. Yes, the pair had disobeyed Betty, er, God, but the damage was done as soon as they gained the forbidden knowledge. And why was it forbidden? My interpretation is unorthodox, to say the least, but I understand the Garden as a level of consciousness, perhaps one that humans lost as we evolved to become more dependent on conceptualization. Can we return to that consciousness, at least occasionally? Do we want to? And what does knowledge of good and evil have to do with it?

I have my own answers to those questions, but I think the value of the myth lies in one's own exploration of it, so I'll leave that to you if you want to give it a go.

In *The Power of Myth* PBS series with Bill Moyers, Joseph Campbell proposed that the angel with a flaming sword assigned to keep humans out of the Garden is Manjusri, the Buddhist bodhisattva of wisdom. This isn't something that the author(s) of the Eden story would have thought of, because Manjusri didn't make his debut as an iconic archetype of wisdom until early in the first millennium CE. I understand the Garden of Eden story is believed to have been composed early in the first millennium BCE, although it probably was based on an older Mesopotamian myth.

Still, Manjusri is an interesting addition. The iconic Manjusri often is depicted holding the sword of discerning wisdom, which cuts through ego, ignorance and the entanglements of conceptual views. Sometimes the sword is in flames, which can represent light or transformation. As well as cutting obstacles and defilements away, the sword also "cuts" separated things into one, by cutting dualism, the self-other dichotomy and whatever else separates us from the Great Ineffable Whatever.

As the angel with a flaming sword, then, the bodhisattva of wisdom would represent both the barrier that keeps us out of the Garden as well as the means to re-enter it.

* * *

For now we see through a glass, darkly; but then face to face: now I know in part; but then shall I know even as also I am known. 1 Corinthians 13:12 KJV

* * *

Reinhold Niebuhr (1892-1971) was an enormously influential American theologian and public intellectual. I'm explaining this for any young people who might have gotten this far in the book. The older folks probably remember him, if only because he's the guy who wrote the Serenity Prayer. His obituary in *Time* magazine called him "the greatest Protestant theologian in America since Jonathan Edwards." He also played a major role in shaping mid-20th century liberalism, from the eras of Franklin Roosevelt to that of John F. Kennedy.

As a theologian, Niebuhr often referred to the doctrine of original sin, although his take on original sin was not exactly how I remember it. I dimly recollect being told that all humans are born sinful because of Adam and Eve's transgression in the Garden, which was the original sin, which is why we needed Christ to redeem us. In researching this topic I realize now there have been many views of original sin going way back, some of which are quite sophisticated. What I remembered is the preschool version.

Once central to Christian theology, by Niebuhr's time it seemed even Christian theology had grown disinterested in original sin. Modernism had begotten optimism in the capacity of society, and the self, to be so much better if we just could get our act together. We are infinitely self-improvable. Original sin was a downer; people wanted to believe they had been born with boundless potential, not demerits.

But Niebuhr saw a fly in the utopian ointment. History shows us, he said,

> ...no matter how wide the perspectives which the human mind may reach, how broad the loyalties which the human imagination may conceive, how universal the community which human statecraft may organize, or how pure the aspirations of the saintliest idealists may be, there is no level of human or social achievement in which there is not some corruption of inordinate self-love. [*The Children of Light and the Children of Darkness*, 1944]

We are born, Niebuhr said, with a desire for self-fulfillment and self-realization. Yet in this desire is a hidden paradox, for only in giving of oneself to others is the self fulfilled. Unconscious of this paradox, humans nearly always pursue gain instead of giving. We have a "darkly unconscious sense" of our own insignificance in the grand scheme of things, he said, and we compensate by pursuing self-glorification, which inevitably encroaches on the self-glorification of others.

More Niebuhr:

> Actually there is a great mystery in the fact that man, who is so created that he cannot fulfill his life except in his fellowmen, and who has some consciousness of this law of love in his very nature, to nevertheless seek so persistently to make his fellowmen the tools of his desires and the objects of his ambitions. If we try to explain this tendency toward self-love, we can find various plausible explanations. We can say it is

due to the fact that man exists at the juncture of nature and spirit, of freedom and necessity. Being a weak creature, he is anxious for his life; and being a resourceful creature, armed with the guile of spirit, he seeks to overcome his insecurity by the various instruments which are placed at his disposal by the resources of his freedom. But inevitably, the security which he seeks for himself is bought at the price of other men's security. Being an insignificant creature with suggestions of great significance in the stature of his freedom, man uses his strength to hide his weakness and thus falls into the evil of the lust for power and self-idolatry. [*Discerning the Signs of the Times*, 1946]

Niebuhr recalled the Garden of Eden myth and the way the snake tempted Eve by suggesting that God wanted to deny humans the power of wisdom, a power that would make them God's equal. For Niebuhr, this is not something that happened only in a mythical past, however. Every human generation has succumbed to the same temptation by seeking power and self-glorification, he said. "Man's situation tempts to evil, provided man is unwilling to accept the peculiar weakness of his creaturely life, and is unable to find the ultimate source and end of his existence beyond himself," Niebuhr wrote in *Discerning the Signs of the Times*. Time and time again, lack of faith — trust in something beyond the limited self — combined with pride do us in.

Back in Chapter 2 I quoted Karen Armstrong — "A myth was never intended as an accurate account of a historical event; it was *something that had in some sense happened once but that also happens all the time.*" Myths have value because they provide insight into things that happen all the time. That's how they are meant to be understood, and here is an example.

And here's a paradox: Religion easily can become just another expression of this same pride and lack of faith. It can be used as a medium through which people seek self-glorification and power over others. In Niebuhr's view, genuine faith is not about armoring oneself in correct dogma, assuming perfect knowledge of God, and lording it over others with different views. Genuine faith acknowledges one's limits and places trust in a God beyond human understanding. The role of religion, Niebuhr said, is not to give us a sense of infallibility but a sense of humility.

"A genuine faith resolves the mystery of life by the mystery of God," he wrote.

Ironically, the "Bible-believing Christian" who is so certain he knows exactly what God thinks that he wants God's opinion written into law and will consider no compromise on the matter has fallen for the same old bait. He has been tempted by the snake — representing his own ego — and has succumbed to the Great Temptation, the original sin.

* * *

Niebuhr's advice about resolving the mystery of life by the mystery of God doesn't work for a Buddhist, of course, but Buddhists reading this might recognize some common threads between Niebuhr's understanding of original sin and the Buddha's Four Noble Truths.

The Four Noble Truths propose that life is *dukkha*, a Sanskrit/Pali word often translated as "suffering," but whose meaning is closer to "unable to satisfy" or "stressful." We seek self-fulfillment but go about it the wrong way, through self-glorification. Everything we grasp to make us feel secure or happy will, sooner or later, disappoint us, because all phenomena are temporary. Thus, life is dukkha — unable to satisfy.

Instead of original sin, however, the Buddha showed us primordial ignorance — of ourselves, of the nature of our existence. Our ignorance, our mistaken views of self-and-other, give rise to greed, hatred, and all the other impulses that drive us to harm others and ourselves. Our insatiable cravings and self-clinging cannot be stopped by force of will, however, but only by direct and intimate insight into the truth about ourselves and our circumstance. Realizing this insight, the Buddha said, requires dedicated practice, and he taught the Eightfold Path to guide that practice. And much about practice of the Path leads to giving of oneself to others, which Niebuhr called the only means of genuine self-fulfillment. [lvi]

Whether you are a Christian or a Buddhist or following another spiritual path, walking that path requires a willingness to acknowledge that your current understanding of everything is clouded — seen through a glass darkly, as Saint Paul said. It also requires a willingness to remain open to new understanding. Certitude is a dead end.

In Zen, it's said that a successful student has three attributes — great faith, great doubt and great determination. "Faith" here refers to trust and confidence, in the practice and in oneself, not in belief. Doctrines act as guides on the path and are not the absolute truth in themselves. *The hand pointing to the moon is not the moon.* Determination is the personal commitment one makes to practice.

"Doubt" is a little harder to explain. To doubt is to neither believe nor disbelieve. To doubt is to acknowledge that there is something not understood. In this case, it's a willingness to relinquish certitude and appreciate that nothing is as it seems. It's also working with scriptures and doc-trines that make no intellectual sense but are *intuitively* brilliant. Many of us must re-learn learning.

Merely *believing in* any of it is pointless, though. Doubt is a path; belief is a prop.

* * *

Back in 2007 I wrote a series of posts for The Mahablog titled "The Wisdom of Doubt," which turned out pretty well. People still ask about it. Like any productive writer I recycle my own work all the time, and I've cannibalized bits of "Wisdom" to re-use in this book, although I really haven't repeated all that much of it. It's still online if you want to read it.[lvii]

I wrote "Wisdom of Doubt" because I'd come to believe the world suffered from too much certitude, and not just the religious parts. As a culture, somewhere along the line we all got the idea that having rigidly fixed beliefs and opinions is a virtue. For example, a politician who expressed one view in 2008, or even 1998, and another today is at risk of being called a flip-flopper.

Do we really want to be governed by people utterly incapable of changing their minds? Who have, in effect, stopped learning and thinking?

And while we're at it, let's give ourselves permission to sometimes say three little words — *I don't know* — without feeling that we're admitting to a fault or a weakness.

While working on the series I came across this definition of *doubt* from an online Catholic encyclopedia:

> A state in which the mind is suspended between two contra-dictory propositions and unable to assent to either of them.
> ... Doubt is opposed to certitude, or the adhesion of the mind to a proposition without misgiving as to its truth.

If you are a spiritual seeker, being suspended between contradic-tory propositions — and I don't know why we have to be limited to just *two* contradictory propositions — is a great place to be. It is only in a state of not knowing that great insight is possible.

I also like the definition of certitude — *adhesion of the mind to a proposition without misgiving as to its truth*. You're stuck there, in other words. Note that the non-religious are just as liable to develop certitude as the religious; they just develop certitude about different things.

This reminds me of a great saying I heard years ago — *A man with one watch knows what time it is. A man with two watches is never sure.* Being sure doesn't mean you're right; being not sure means you're more likely to seek the truth, or at least get closer to it.

Zen actually came up with ways to instill doubt, in case you don't have enough. They're called *koans*, those enigmatic questions about one hand clapping and whatnot. Most koans present some kind of impossible paradox that cannot be resolved through linear, logical thought. In formal koan contemplation one works with the koan in a non-conceptual way, taking it into one's bones, keeping it in one's awareness, but not trying to "figure it out." The process has a way of dismantling one's assumptions about what is and what isn't, replacing certitude with doubt. *There is resolution*, although it's hard to say if the student resolves the koan or the koan resolves the student.

* * *

Not unlike a spiritual seeker, a scientist must doubt. A dedicated scientist must always be willing to question assumptions and adjust his ideas in light of new evidence. The scientist works mostly with rational mind rather than with intuitive mind, with logos rather than mythos, although I suspect intuition plays a part now and then.

The significance of scientific rationalism is that it changed *how* people interpret the world, not just what they knew about it. It allowed people to comprehend many things they could not comprehend before.

Scientific rationalism has done humanity a lot of good. However, it posed a challenge to religion that much of religion has failed. Too much of religion responded to the challenge of science by trying to *compete* with it. Instead of marking the distinction between the wisdom of mythos and the knowledge of logos, religion tried to claim that it can be scientific and factual, too. But, really, it *can't*. Not without making itself ridiculous.

The truth is, most of the time religion is its own worst enemy, and scriptural literalism is a major stumbling block. Some religious conservatives fight science tooth and nail, mostly because they think that denying the literal truth of scripture is denying God. But, if anything, just the opposite is true. Literalism makes scripture absurd and God a finite creature of human imagination. It is scriptural literalism, not science, that denies God.

The shame of it is that religion doesn't need to compete with science to be valid in its own way. Determining scientific factuality is not what it's for.

The late Stephen Jay Gould, paleontologist, evolutionary biologist and author, proposed the principle of "nonoverlapping magisteria," which says that science and religion each inhabits its own legitimate domain of teaching authority. "The net of science covers the empirical universe: what is it made of (fact) and why does it work this way (theory)," Gould wrote in 1997. "The net of religion extends over questions of moral meaning and value. These two magisteria do not overlap, nor do they encompass all inquiry (consider, for starters, the magisterium of art and the meaning of beauty)."

If you've been reading this book you will know I don't agree that religion primarily is about moral meaning and value, but I do generally agree with the principle of nonoverlapping magisteria. Science and *nonliteral* religion do different kinds of work and obtain different kinds of results, and that shouldn't be a problem. In math class you calculate the number of apples; in biology class you study apple trees; in home economics you make apple pie.

However, there's nothing at all wrong with admiring each other's efforts. Reading about neuroscience actually helped me understand Yogacara philosophy, discussed in Chapter 4, a little better. But most of the time the answers provided by science and religion will be different, which doesn't mean one is true and the other false. It means one must take into account what the answers are true *of*.

Scriptural literalism denies both scientific and religious truth. This is something that progressive and not-literalist priests, pastors, rabbis, imams, ministers and theologians understand perfectly well. They would change the course of religion if they could, but there's a lot in their way.

Today, in many parts of the world right-wing religious extremists have made common cause with right-wing political extremists to push back against modernity and democracy. They've got money and momentum. Some of them have well-armed militias. Many have the tacit approval and protection of government, even when they become violent. Sometimes they *are* the government.

Progressive-liberal religion has no such support. Progressive politics mostly keeps progressive religion at arm's length, in spite of western progressivism's historical roots in Christianity and Judaism. And the true believers of New Atheism, which denies that religion is anything *but* fundamentalism, aren't helping.

And it's also the case that many liberal religious people are uncomfortable telling others their doctrines are wrong. Conservative reli-

gious people rarely have such qualms. So the playing field is not exactly
level.

* * *

I am for freedom of religion and against all maneuvers to
bring about a legal ascendancy of one sect over another.
[Thomas Jefferson to Elbridge Gerry, 1799]

History, I believe, furnishes no example of a priest-ridden
people maintaining a free civil government. [Thomas Jefferson to Alexander von Humboldt, 1813]

* * *

In February 2014 former congressman and House Majority Leader
Tom Delay (Republican-Texas) told interviewer Matthew Hagee that God
wrote the U.S. Constitution. People have forgotten, Delay said, that "God
created this nation [and] that He wrote the Constitution, that it's based on
biblical principles."

You'll have to ask the former Congressman exactly what biblical
principles are involved in determining that Congress has power to levy
taxes and that the President is commander-in-chief of the military. Of
course, the truth is that the fellows who wrote the Constitution deliberate-
ly left all mention of God out of it, which was unusual for an 18th century
official document.

The authors of the Constitution wrote it the way they did because
they knew European history very well, and they knew that Europe had
suffered all kinds of war and political instability because of religion.

Particularly after Martin Luther kicked off the Reformation and
the Catholic Church had competition, religion got deeply involved in partisan politics because of the advantages of living under a monarch who
favored your church. The "established" church received tax money to
maintain itself and the ability to influence policies to favor itself. To obtain
establishment, clergy corrupted themselves shamelessly, plotting and
scheming to gain political advantage, and soldiers slaughtered one another
over whether they would be ruled by a Catholic or a Protestant. Many
people came to America to escape all that.

But how would the new United States of America avoid falling into the same pattern? James Madison and the other authors of the Constitution came up with an elegant answer. In the very first clause of the very

First Amendment, they deprived the federal government of the power to "establish" religion, which in the language of 18th-century English common law meant establishing an official state religion, or favoring one religion over all others. Even if, for example, every single member of Congress, the President, and all nine Supreme Court justices happened to be Lutheran, the government may not pass laws or enact policies favoring Lutheranism. If there is no advantage to be gained by scheming and plotting and fighting to take over the government, the Founders figured, then religious factions would be much less likely to scheme and plot and start fights to take over the government. Brilliant, yes?

On the American Right, the establishment clause doesn't exist. Or if it exists, it isn't important. Or if it is important, it doesn't say what it says. If backed into a corner, they will sneer that us liberals (read: elite snotty communist atheist America haters) are really in love with that establishment clause, aren't we? Conservatives like to skip the first clause and go directly to the second clause, on the free exercise of religion, because (in their minds) they are all about freedom.

For example, in a much derided speech delivered in Houston in 2010,[lviii] former senator Rick Santorum tried his best to explain away half of Thomas Jefferson's "wall of separation of church and state" — "Jefferson's 'wall of separation' was describing how the First Amendment was designed to protect churches from the government and nothing more," Santorum said. No, Senator, it also was designed to protect government from interference by churches.

If you have even a casual knowledge of Jefferson, you ought to know he didn't trust religious institutions as far as he could throw them and strongly believed they should be kept out of having a say in government. This is not to say that Jefferson wanted religion banned from public view; not at all. But he believed strongly that (1) government should not show a preference to one sect over another, and in his autobiography and letters he made it clear that he did not think Christianity should be shown favoritism over non-Christian religions; and (2) "believers" must not be allowed to govern according to their particular religious beliefs.

Jefferson's buddy James Madison, chief author of the Constitution and Bill of Rights, was by all accounts on the same page as Jefferson where church and state were concerned. Madison once said "religion & Govt will both exist in greater purity, the less they are mixed together." Anyone who says that the Founders intended the United States to be governed by Christianity is either ignorant of history or lying.

The truth is, religious freedom in the United States rests on both the establishment and free exercise clauses, because you can't have one without the other. There's no such thing as a one-sided wall.

Santorum seems to think that "government" has some kind of existence separate from the people elected to it and employed by it. But it does not. "Government" by itself cannot so much as pull up its own socks. Everything government does is actually being done by the people either elected to it or employed by it, and if people gain control of government for the purpose of promoting their own religious agendas, that's an example of both church interfering with government and government interfering with religious freedom. And in American history, it's only when "church" has interfered with government that government — in promoting a sectarian agenda — has been inclined to interfere with church by trampling on the free exercise of *other* religious faiths as well as the freedom to not be religious at all.

The letter in which Jefferson coined "wall of separation" was in response to Connecticut Baptists complaining that their state required them to pay taxes to support the Congregationalist Church. This is government interfering with the free exercise of religion, but it happened because back when Connecticut was a colony Congregationalists dominated the colonial government. Originally the establishment clause applied only to the federal government, so Connecticut as a state still had the power to establish a church. The 14th Amendment provided that states may not infringe of the rights of United States citizens, including their religious rights, so today states may not establish religions, either.

Most of the Supreme Court decisions that stopped the practice of reciting prayers in public school classrooms and assemblies were responses to suits brought by people of minority faiths. *Engel v. Vitale* (1962) was filed by Jewish families with children in public school who objected to the prayers their children were being compelled to recite. Mr. Schempp of *Abington School District v. Schempp* (1963) was a Unitarian Universalist. The more recent *Santa Fe Independent School Dist. v. Doe* (2000), which involved prayers read over loudspeakers at Texas high school football games, was filed by two families, one Catholic and one Mormon, who were offended by the religious beliefs expressed in the prayers.

These court cases provide examples of government interfering with the free exercise of religion, but not in the way the Right understands it. Right-wingers see them as the federal government interfering with the right of children to pray in school, which is nonsense. Instead, they are examples of a dominant religious group using government (in this case, public schools) to trample on the free exercise of minority religions, and the Court's decisions protected genuine free exercise by upholding the establishment clause, made applicable to the states by the 14th Amendment.

* * *

There's a lot about the public culture of right-wing Christian religiosity in the U.S. that is remarkably un-Christian. If you were to have learned everything you knew about religion from the American Right, you'd think God not only wrote the Constitution but also established and ordained free-market capitalism. War, greed, and hatred are noble, peace is for wimps, and nothing is more important to Jesus than seeing to it gays can't marry and women can't have abortions.

This is one of the hallmarks of religion-as-identity, discussed in the last chapter. When religion becomes one's tribal identity rather than one's spiritual path, the more peaceful and compassionate doctrines of that religion are among the first casualties. When doctrine can be twisted around to support ideology and bias, it will be so twisted; otherwise, um, what Sermon on the Mount?

And as much as I, and maybe you, poke fun at the U.S. religious Right, they share most of the traits of violent religious factions that were discussed in the last chapter.

Needless to say, if this crew ever gains control of all three branches of government in the U.S., we can all kiss civil liberty — including religious freedom — goodbye. I don't think that's likely to happen in my lifetime, or beyond that, as demographic trends seem to be turning against them. But as power and influence slip away from them, it's very possible we'll see an increase in right-wing domestic terrorism. The elements usually found in violent religious groups — in particular, a holy cause and a fanatical grievance — certainly are present in America's religious right wing. We'd be very naïve to assume *it can't happen here.*

* * *

Now, a word to activist atheists: You're starting to scare me, too. Some of you seem to be just as stuffed with righteousness and certitude as the religious Right.

Atheists are just as likely as anyone else to develop bad cases of dogmatism, along with orthodoxies and tribalism. One of the tell-tale signs of a closed mind is an inability to even recognize, much less comprehend, arguments that don't match a rigid and limited set of pre-formed cognitive models, and I run into that a lot with atheists. Often they refuse to acknowledge any definition of God or any form of religious expression except for the most ridiculously infantile. The ambiguous nature of existence (see Chapter 4) usually eludes them, and they can't be bothered trying to understand it; stuff either *exists* or it *doesn't exist*. And faith is "belief without evidence" because Christopher Hitchens said so.

By now you should know I don't give a hoo-haw whether someone believes in God or not. I think atheism shouldn't be a handicap to being elected to public office. I agree that atheists can be just as moral as people who believe in God. I'd love to rid the world of proselytizing. All school children should learn about evolution in biology class.

I am not your enemy, in other words. Yet we seem to have *issues*, don't we?

I realize that religion has genuinely harmed a lot of people, and people have a right to their feelings about it. But you don't appease ignorance with more ignorance. Instead of endlessly whacking at the strawman religion in your heads, it would be much more useful if activist atheists targeted the literalists, dogmatists, and others who use religion as a moral cover for bigotry. Dear atheists, I would join you in that. You might be surprised at how many other religious people would join you in that.

But first, open your minds and become skeptics in the true sense of the word.

In his book *The Unpersuadables*, Will Storr describes a Skeptics convention in Manchester, UK. The Skeptics are a group of people dedicated to science and reason, and they take particular delight in refuting all forms of *quackitude* — psychics, homeopathy, ghosts, God. "Their main hobby seems to be not believing in things," Storr writes. He also describes them as "knights of hard intellect whose ultimate goal is a world free of superstitious thinking."

Storr shares their disbeliefs, for the most part, but finds the group depressing for reasons he can't quite put his finger on. He interviews conventioneers and finds many haven't personally studied either the things they debunk or those they approve, but they could cite studies they'd heard about but hadn't read to support their positions. Storr's description of the convention makes it seem mostly about people congratulating each other for joining the Smart People tribe. Storr continues,

> There is a famous quote by William James, who spoke of the
> scientific gains that can be made by paying attention to "the

dust-cloud of exceptional observations" that floats around "the accredited and orderly facts of every science." What if some young academic who is interested in an esoteric subject such as homeopathy or ESP is intimidated by the roar of the crowd into ignoring his vocation? Maybe, in among all this junk science, some crucial anomaly exists, the study of which could lead to a fantastic breakthrough? But now it won't happen because reason's fightback is too fierce, too gloating, too much of a threat to a young scientist's reputation. To be a Skeptic seems to involve signing up to a predetermined rainbow of unbeliefs. What if it slips into dogma?

Indeed, the history of science is well larded with stories of groundbreaking scientists who had to fight the scientific establishment to be heard. These stories always seem unreal in retrospect, but they happened.

Just one example — I'm thinking now of Ignaz Semmelweis (1818-1865), who discovered that incidents of puerperal fever, a postpartum infection that killed many women after giving birth, could be drastically reduced if physicians merely cleaned their hands before touching the laboring mother. Medical science of the day didn't know about germs, but Semmelweis proposed that some kind of invisible particles on doctors' hands spread the infection, and he produced impressive data showing that his hand-washing procedure made a significant difference in postpartum mortality rates.

The medical establishment rejected Semmelweis's proposal, however, because it didn't jibe with the accepted and orderly facts of the day. Other doctors dismissed Semmelweis's unseen particles as a fairy tale; obviously, what can't be seen doesn't exist, they said. Doctors also were insulted by Semmelweis's suggestion that their hands were dirty. Semmelweis became *persona non grata* at doctors' conventions. His health deteriorated and his behavior became erratic. He was committed to an asylum for the mentally disturbed at the age of 47 and beaten to death by guards a few days later.

And a few years after that, Louis Pasteur (1822-1895) proposed germ theory, partly drawing on Semmelweis's work. Although Semmelweis had no idea the invisible particles were living organisms, they weren't a fairy tale.

You might think that can't happen *now*. In *The Righteous Mind*, Jonathan Haidt writes about E.O. Wilson, who is considered by many to be the world's most distinguished living biologist. Back in the 1970s, Haidt said, Wilson published a book that proposed that human nature and behavior had been shaped by natural selection. He also proposed what Haidt also believes to be true, that our moral judgments originate in our emotions, and reason is then drafted to craft a narrative to justify that judgment. Wilson's proposals were utterly outside acceptably progressive social-scientific opinion at the time, however. Haidt writes,

> He was harassed and excoriated in print and in public. He was called a fascist, which justified (for some) the charge that he was a racist, which justified (for some) the attempt to stop him from speaking in public. Protesters who tried to disrupt one of his scientific talks rushed the stage and chanted, "Racist Wilson, you can't hide, we charge you with genocide."

Mind you, this antipathy to Wilson's proposal was coming from academia, not the general public. And it happened because the man had proposed human behavior had been shaped by natural selection. How the protesters got from there to genocide I have no idea. And the moral is that *no collection of human beings is immune to herd mentalities and groupthink.*

Going by dictionary definitions, skepticism is synonymous with doubt. It is not knee-jerk, dogmatic disbelief, but "an attitude of doubt or a disposition to incredulity," according to Merriam-Webster.

How do we distinguish dogmatic disbelief from genuine doubt?

Doubt is dispassionate. Doubt does not get tangled in ego or self-identity. At the same time, however, doubt is personal, not social, because doubt rarely can stand up to peer pressure. Peer pressure nearly always turns doubt into a dogma, either of belief or disbelief.

Doubt has no gurus. Doubt doesn't join Doubter's Clubs.

Doubt is willing to say things like, "I don't know," "I'm not sure I understand your argument," and "I could be wrong." And mean it.

Doubt is willing to stay open to new perspectives. Doubt does not shy away from clarification, if it comes, but after clarification it remains open to *further* clarification. There is no final answer.

Maybe what the world needs now is love, but it could also use a lot more doubt.

I realize that people often are uncomfortable with doubt. I think our brains are wired to attach to certainties, to *know*, even if what we know is all wrong. Maybe our ancient ancestors evolved certainty-seeking brains because if they were too blasé about things they didn't know, those things might eat them. But in modern times, certainty is way overrated.

Eric Hoffer wrote, "To be in possession of an absolute truth is to have a net of familiarity spread over the whole of eternity. There are no surprises and no unknowns. All questions have already been answered, all decisions made, all eventualities foreseen." Certainty, true belief — or true disbelief — is like a mental security blanket. But certainty doesn't actually make us safer, especially when we go to war with each other over clashing certainties.

So, maintaining a state of dispassionate doubt isn't easy. It may take some practice. Buddhist meditation actually is pretty good at growing and maintaining dispassionate doubt, but only if you are willing to stick with it for, oh, about the rest of your life. It's not a quick fix. I have to say, though, that while I still cling to some certainties, I'm a lot better at not knowing things than I used to be.

* * *

"Doubt is our saving grace." — overheard at a Zen center

* * *

Once I went to a lecture on Islam. The speaker was a physician and a member of a local Sunni mosque. This was during the first Gulf War, and we'd all just learned the word *jihad*. The speaker said that jihad could refer to a "holy war," but it could also refer to any spiritual struggle. "And in my experience," he said, "the real struggle, the real jihad, is with yourself."

Take it from an old Zen student; these were wise words. *The real struggle is with yourself.*

The real struggle is also *about* yourself, or about who and what you are in relation to everything else. We all experience our lives and ourselves in a context of cultural, political and social conditions. These conditions are a big part of the conceptual box we all live in, the box of who we think we are and what we think life is supposed to be.

This may seem odd advice, coming from a Zen student. We're supposed to believe the self is an illusion, right? But in fact we're not supposed to *believe* anything. The practice is about personal realization, and a big part of that is personal realization of the nature of the self. This is done by looking into the self, not by believing a bunch of doctrines about it.

Here in the West most of us like to pretend we're all completely autonomous and independent person-units, but that's not so. Until we've at least perceived the box, we're just kidding ourselves. And sometimes when we do perceive we're living in a box, we "save" ourselves by climbing into another box. When you hear of someone swinging from one extreme political view to another, that's what happened.

There's a science fiction plot device about artificial realities, in which the characters are either dreaming or in some kind of induced fantasy state. And they realize what they are experiencing isn't real, so they wake up, or think they do. But what has really happened is that they are experiencing a new dream-fantasy of being awake and safe, when in fact they are still dreaming and the monsters are still about to harvest their bodily fluids. I know I've seen variations of that plot on *Star Trek* and *X-Files* and probably other places.

"Real" life can be like that. We sleepwalk through life dreaming that we're awake. We wise up to an illusion and replace it with another one. We ditch a belief system and embrace its equally fallacious opposite.

This happens because we go through life frantically grabbing at things to make ourselves feel "real" and substantive, and those things include dogmas of both belief and disbelief and in-group and out-group identities of all sorts. These become the landscapes of the dream-fantasy life that we mistake for reality. If at some point cognitive dissonances snap and we realize something we believe isn't true, most of the time we quickly replace it with another belief to patch up the hole in the dream-fantasy box. If we feel betrayed by a belief, very likely we will rebound to its opposite — from Left to Right, say, or from religion to anti-religion.

But within all of our contexts, connections and beliefs, where do we find the self? Who is the dreamer?

Back in my college days my sociology professor challenged the class to identify ourselves without reference to a relationship. We were to avoid describing ourselves as the child of our parents, for example, or the employee of an employer, or a student at the university. And none of us could do it. We could give our names and physical descriptions, but we couldn't say anything about "me" — the "inner" person we thought we were — without placing ourselves in some kind of niche in some kind of social system. And I bet you can't, either.

In other words, we cannot be who we are without everything else being what it is. And what does that say about our own autonomy? What does that say about personal freedom or individual liberty? We are not the autonomous person-units we think we are.

In this book I've cited people — Carl Jung, Erich Fromm, Hannah Arendt and Eric Hoffer — who witnessed the rise of the massive totalitarian states of the 20th century. And in much of their writing they addressed the question of how people, as individuals and nations, are seduced into accepting totalitarianism. No nation ever reached the collective conclusion that it *wanted* to be under the thumb of a ruthless dictator, yet it happens.

President George W. Bush used to go around saying things like "Whenever people are given a choice in the matter, they prefer lives of freedom to lives of fear." And "Free people are not drawn to violent and malignant ideologies." But that's hogwash. Free people choose to be fearful every day. Free people are drawn to violent and malignant ideologies every day. There's no easier way to unite a crowd than to whip them up into a state of rage or fear of some little-understood Other, and once you've done that violent and malignant ideologies are but a step behind.

And if you get people whipped up enough, they will trade freedom for safety, or what they think is safety, nearly every time. This is true whether what they fear or despise is real or imaginary.

And it's often the case that as we run from things that frighten us we stampede straight over a cliff. Totalitarianism can take many forms, as can zealotry and fanaticism, and people fall into these things because they don't recognize them for what they are.

The 20th century taught people to fear Big Government, but that fear appears to have blinded a lot of people to the infinite other ways humans enslave and oppress each other, for which government actually can be a remedy. The 20th century taught people to embrace capitalism over communism, and in their anti-communist zeal many willfully overlook the many ways capitalism can be abusive, too. We may wake up one day slaves to some global corporate oligarchy, and our governments will be too weak or compromised to secure our rights and protect us.

Likewise, people who see humanity divided neatly between religion/superstition versus science/reason have little understanding of religion or reason, never mind humanity. Not all religion is blind belief. Most of those who thump their chests and declare themselves to be rational thinkers are living in a dream-fantasy state. The fanatically dogmatic anti-religionist is no more awake to reality than the religious fundamentalist.

The only way to inoculate yourself from being swallowed into the herd is to truly come home to yourself and intimately experience who you are. As Eric Hoffer said, "Only the individual who has come to terms with his self can have a dispassionate attitude toward the world." Otherwise you're going to be perpetually grabbing for something Out There to give definition and substance to the box you live in. This is true whether the thing you grab for is religion or libertarianism or something else.

Carl Jung wrote in *The Undiscovered Self* that a person requires "the inner, transcendent experience which alone can protect him from the otherwise inevitable submersion in the mass. Merely intellectual and even moral insight into the stultification and moral irresponsibility of the mass man is a negative recognition only and amounts to not much more than a wavering on the road to the atomization of the individual."

In other words, embracing the right ideology or the correct philosophy will not save you. This is true even if your ideology is all about Freedom. Without intimate experience of the self you'll still just be an ant in a groupthink ant hill, no matter how many times you've read *Atlas Shrugged*.

Let me add that much about contemporary life is making us more estranged from ourselves, not less. We are sorting ourselves into ideological tribes and marketing niches. We multitask and juggle and compartmentalize ourselves and our lives umpteen ways. Thanks to technology, our jobs are eating our personal lives. We can catch up on office email without even getting out of bed, after all. I think some of us are not so much a self as a grab bag of identities — e.g., *accountant, mother, independent voter, consumer, Generation X-er, white suburbanite, country music fan.*

The next questions: How do we intimately experience ourselves? *Who are we? What are we missing? How do we reconnect?*

We all need to step outside our everyday life sometimes. We need time to reflect and be alone with ourselves. We need to drop our identities and reconnect to the person who was there before the identities took up our inner space. We need a means to cultivate what is within as much as what is without.

That is a role that religion has filled in the past and can fill now, if we can get over the idea that religion is about joining tribes and believing things. Buddhist meditation and mindfulness practices are very much about intimate experience, but intimate experience can be found in other religious traditions also. And meditation/contemplation doesn't have to have a religious context, of course. Sometimes clearing one's head and taking a mindful walk in the woods can do wonders.

Just don't think of your mindfulness/spiritual/whatever practice as a self-improvement project or another kind of identity. Think in terms of releasing everything and returning to the source. I'll leave it to you to determine what the "source" is.

I realize I tend to kick props out from under people. In the course of this book I've suggested you're probably kidding yourself about everything. The world around you is a mental fabrication. You may or may not exist. Your holy scriptures are bad translations of scraps of old texts mostly written by people you never heard of. Your rational mind isn't all that rational. Even atheists and scientists can succumb to groupthink and dogma. There *may* be a God, but if so, God isn't God — or, at least, not whatever God you imagine.

Let's go back to Thanissaro Bhikkhu's question from the chapter on scriptures — *Where can you place your trust?*

So there you are, some bone and flesh and senses, trying to muddle through a little blip of a life somewhere in the vast expanse of time and space. And the smartest, most successful people you know are in exactly the same fix. *Where can you place your trust?*

I'm not sure there's any one right answer. And if I did have the one right answer, and told you what it is, you shouldn't believe me, anyway. Wisdom is not found in believing what you've been told but in realizing it for yourself.

The alternative to working with this question is to be stuck in groupthink and dogma and mental security blankets, whether you are religious or not. You might start by examining yourself to determine where you *do* place your trust, and then giving some serious thought to whether that trust-place really is trustworthy, or whether it's a place you stick to because it's comfortable or flatters your ego.

And I wish you all the best with that.

I said at the beginning of the book that I don't think everyone has to be religious. It's an individual thing. For myself, I have no use for religion that's nothing but a crutch or a band-aid, or one that provides sweet, fluffy beliefs to help one avoid dealing honestly with the realities of life and death. But not all religion is like that. It *can* be a challenge and a guide and a source of genuine strength and wisdom, if you are willing to take it on.

I also said at the beginning of the book that I hoped to challenge your ideas about religion, whatever they are. I've been writing long enough to know that some people will stop reading this book as soon as they realize it isn't the book they expected it to be. For that matter, it isn't exactly the book I expected to write, but I had some things to say that no one else seemed to be saying. And here we are. Maybe some perspectives will broaden.

And if we can stop arguing about whether God exists, and stop giving the most fanatical and literalist religionists exclusive rights to speak for God (whether he exists or not) in mass media, the world at least will be a less annoying place.

And to all of you, *metta.*

Endnotes

Chapter 1: The Religion Problem

[i] You can read about this at http://www.pewforum.org/ 2014/01/14/religious-hostilities-reach-six-year-high/ .

Chapter 2: Defining Religion

[ii] His Holiness the 14th Dalai Lama, *Beyond Religion: Ethics for a Whole World* (Houghton Mifflin Harcourt, 2011), from Chapter 1.

[iii] In the Kalama Sutta (this is found in the Pali Tipitika, Anguttara Nikaya, 3:65) the historical Buddha is recorded as saying that one must not accept anything as truth just because it's written in scripture. So there. Of course, we could always wander in circles wondering if we should accept this advice as truth.

[iv] http://buddhism.about.com/b/2010/01/04/lets-forgive-brit-hume. htm

[v] *Vedanta* refers to particular spiritual traditions that emerged from the Vedic religions of India and now are considered part of Hinduism.

Chapter 3: Spiritual Is Religious

[vi] I swear I'm not making this up. http://www.rawstory.com/ rs/2014/01/07/pat-robertson-global-warming-is-a-scam-because-there-are-no-suvs-on-jupiter/

[vii] Pew Research Religion and Public Life Project, "Public's Views on Human Evolution," December 30, 2013. Online at http://www.pewforum.org/2013/12/30/publics-views-on-human-evolution/

[viii] The Stanford Encyclopedia of Philosophy is online. It can be interesting if you can get around the academese.

[ix] Sam Harris, "Selfless Consciousness Without Faith," Washingtonpost.com, January 8, 2007. http://www.faithstreet.com/onfaith/2007/01/08/consciousness-without-faith-1/8436

[x] This happened in August 2012.

[xi] There are translations online, if you want to Google for it.

Chapter 4: God and Existence

[xii] If you have studied Buddhism you may be most familiar with the third "world," the world of desire, which is divided into the six realms of the Bhava-chakra, or "wheel of life."

[xiii] Mahayana is large school of Buddhism to which both the Tibetan and Zen traditions belong.

[xiv] You can read about this at http://www.livescience.com/28132-what-is-nothing-physicists-debate.html .

[xv] http://blogs.scientificamerican.com/brainwaves/2013/12/02/why-life-does-not-really-exist/

[xvi] From "Immo," a fascicle in a collection of Dogen's writings titled *Shobogenzo*.

Chapter 5: Iron Age Morality in a Postmodern World

[xvii] Nathanial Frank, "The Narcissism of Today's Homophobia," *Slate*, February 6, 2014. http://www.slate.com/blogs/outward/2014/02/03/bizzle_s_same_love_t he_narcissism_of_today_s_homophobia.html

[xviii] If you're familiar with the story that the Buddha was reluctant to ordain women and had to be talked into it by the disciple Ananda: I understand this story appears in the Pali Vinaya but not in the Sanskrit/Chinese Vinaya. Also, some historians have pointed out that Ananda would still have been a child when the first ordination of women took place. It is suspected that the story about the Buddha's hesitation to ordain women was added to the Pali Vinaya by an unknown (male) editor some time after the Buddha was no longer around to object.

[xix] http://vochoice.org/

[xx] http://www.prochoiceactionnetwork-canada.org/articles/anti-tales.shtml

[xxi] See "U.S. divorce rates for various faith groups, age groups, & geographic areas," ReligiousTolerance.org, http://www.religioustolerance.org/chr_dira.htm ; Kevin Drum, "Teen Pregnancy Is Higher in Red States than in Blue States," *Mother Jones*, February 18, 2012, http://www.motherjones.com/kevin-drum/2012/02/teen-pregnancy-higher-red-states-blue-states

[xxii] "Abortion in Latin America: Miscarriages of Justice," *The Economist,* July 8, 2013. http://www.economist.com/news/americas/21579065-brutal-farce-el-salvador-highlights-regional-failing-miscarriages-justice

[xxiii] World Health Organization, "Facts and Figures About Abortion in the European Region." http://www.euro.who.int/en/health-topics/Life-stages/sexual-and-reproductive-health/activities/abortion/facts-and-figures-about-abortion-in-the-european-region

[xxiv] Charles Pierce's book *Idiot America: How Stupidity Became a Virtue in the Land of the Free* (Doubleday, 2009) provides a detailed account of the Schiavo incident, if you're interested.

Chapter 6: The Crazy Scripture in the Attic

[xxv] Amir Alexander, "Christianity's original anti-science crusade: The religious order that tried to crush modernity," *Salon,* April 13, 2014. http://www.salon.com/2014/04/13/christianitys_original_anti_science_cr usade_the_religious_order_that_tried_to_crush_modernity/

[xxvi] Online at http://www.accesstoinsight.org/tipitaka/an/an03/an03.065.than.html

[xxvii] See "Lost in Quotation," http://www.accesstoinsight.org/lib/authors/thanissaro/lostinquotation.h tml

[xxviii] http://www.breitbart.com/Big-Hollywood/2014/03/28/Noah-review-brilliantly-sinister-anti-christian-filmmaking

[xxix] http://www.wnd.com/2014/04/noah-revives-ancient-enemy-of-christianity/

[xxx]

http://www.religiondispatches.org/archive/atheologies/7749/noah__cos mos_controversies_not_about_biblical_literalism

Chapter 7: True Believers and Mass Movements

[xxxi] Gary Susman, "Box Office: What's Behind the Surprising Success of 'God's Not Dead'?" *Moviefone,* March 24, 2014. http://news.moviefone.com/2014/03/24/box-office-gods-not-dead/

[xxxii] Eric Brown, "Persecution Pays: How Right-Wing Christian Films Like 'God's Not Dead' And 'Persecuted' Monetize The Persecution Complex," *International Business Times,* April 12, 2014.

http://www.ibtimes.com/persecution-pays-how-right-wing-christian-films-gods-not-dead-persecuted-monetize-1569746

[xxxiii] Miranda Blue, "There Are Two Christian Right Movies Called 'Persecuted' Coming Out This Year," *Right Wing Watch*, February 13, 2014. http://www.rightwingwatch.org/content/there-are-two-christian-right-movies-called-persecuted-coming-out-year

[xxxiv] See Brett Wilkins, "U.S. evangelicals helped write draconian Uganda anti-gay bill," *Digital Journal*, December 23, 2013. http://digitaljournal.com/news/religion/us-evangelicals-helped-write-draconian-uganda-anti-gay-bill/article/364543

[xxxv] The essay is online somewhere, if you want to read it. I have never read the book and do not know what the "last man" refers to. Nor do I care.

[xxxvi] Per economist Paul Krugman, "A zombie idea is a proposition that has been thoroughly refuted by analysis and evidence, and should be dead — but won't stay dead because it serves a political purpose, appeals to prejudices, or both." (Paul Krugman, "Rubio and the Zombies," *The New York Times*, February 15, 2013, p. A27)

[xxxvii] See, for example, Douglas Fischer and *The Daily Climate*, "'Dark Money' Funds Climate Change Denial Efforts," on the website of *Scientific American*, posted December 23, 2013. http://www.scientificamerican.com/article/dark-money-funds-climate-change-denial-effort/

[xxxviii] See Jordan Smith, "Just Say No!" in the *Austin Chronicle*, October 28, 2011. http://www.austinchronicle.com/news/2011-10-28/just-say-no/

[xxxix] Yes, I'm paraphrasing Matthew 20:16.

[xl] "We need somebody to put rat poisoning in Justice Stevens' creme brulee. That's just a joke, for you in the media." — Ann Coulter, Philander Smith College in Little Rock, Arkansas, March 2008.

[xli] "Not that which goeth into the mouth defileth a man; but that which cometh out of the mouth, this defileth a man." (King James Version)

[xlii] Gudo Wafu Nishijima translation

Chapter 8: Religion and Violence

[xliii] Attadanda Sutta, Pali Tipitika, Sutta Nipata 4:15, Andrew Olendzki translation. Online at http://www.accesstoinsight.org/tipitaka/kn/snp/snp.4.15.olen.html

[xliv] Kyaw San Wai, Myanmar's Religious Violence: A Buddhist Siege Mentality at Work?-- Analysis," *Eurasian Review*, February 21, 1014. http://www.eurasiareview.com/21022014-myanmars-religious-violence-buddhist-siege-mentality-work-analysis/

[xlv] Kevin McKiernan, "Buddhist Rampage in Burma," the *Santa Barbara Independent*, March 6, 2014. http://www.independent.com/news/2014/mar/06/buddhist-rampage-burma/

[xlvi] See the Bhikkhu's comments on this at http://www.accesstoinsight.org/lib/authors/thanissaro/gettingmessage.html

[xlvii] If anyone's life story ever cried out to be made into a major motion picture, it's Olcott's.

[xlviii] Robert Kaplan, "Buddha's Savage Peace," *The Atlantic*, September 2009. Online at http://www.theatlantic.com/magazine/archive/2009/09/buddhas-savage-peace/307620/

[xlix] There's a translation online at the Access to Insight website. http://www.accesstoinsight.org/tipitaka/mn/mn.035.than.html

[l] *The Middle Length Discourses of the Buddha: A Translation of the Majjhima Nikaya: New Translation (Teachings of the Buddha)*, translated by Bhikkhu Nanamoli and Bhikkhu Bodhi (Wisdom Publications, 2005).

[li] Candima Sutta, Samyutta Nikaya 2.9, Piyadassi Thera translation. Online at http://www.accesstoinsight.org/tipitaka/sn/sn02/sn02.009.piya.html.

[lii] This translation is online at http://www.accesstoinsight.org/tipitaka/dn/dn.26.0.than.html

[liii] Benjamin Crème, "Raj Patel is not Maitreya, but the World Teacher is here – and needed," *The Guardian* (Comment Is Free), April 20, 2010. http://www.theguardian.com/commentisfree/belief/2010/apr/20/raj-patel-maitreya-world-teacher

[liv] In Zen, "lineage" refers to the lineage of teachers or "Zen masters" — one's teacher, the teacher's teacher, the teacher's teacher's teacher, and so on going back to the historical Buddha and the Buddhas before him. This is a Big Deal in Zen.

[lv] See Nelson Foster and Gary Snyder, "The Fog of World War II: Setting the Record Straight on D.T. Suzuki," *Tricycle,* summer 2010. Online at http://www.tricycle.com/feature/fog-world-war-ii

. See also Jundo Cohen's comments at Sweeping Zen: http://sweepingzen.com/zen-war-author-brian-victorias-unethical-bahavior-jundo-cohen/ ; also Kemmyo Taira Sato, "Brian Victoria and the Question of Scholarship," *The Eastern Buddhist,* 2010, http://www.thezensite.com/ZenEssays/CriticalZen/Question_of_Schola rship.pdf

Chapter 9: The Wisdom of Doubt

[lvi] If you want to learn more about the Four Noble Truths, see "Introduction to the Four Noble Truths" (by me) at About.com — http://buddhism.about.com/od/thefournobletruths/a/The-Four-Noble-Truths.htm

[lvii] http://www.mahablog.com/2007/08/03/the-wisdom-of-doubt-the-series/

[lviii] The speech marked the 50th anniversary of John F. Kennedy's address in the same city, where Kennedy promised that if elected President, he would not use his office to impose Catholic beliefs on the nation. Santorum saw that as a sellout of principle. See the text of the speech at http://www.realclearreligion.org/articles/2012/03/30/it_is_hard_to_be_c atholic_in_public_life.html

Made in the USA
Lexington, KY
04 February 2015